Critical Guides to Spanish Texts

Critical Guides to Spanish Texts

EDITED BY J.E. VAREY AND A.D. DEYERMOND

CARPENTIER

El reino de este mundo

Richard A. Young

Professor of Spanish
University of Alberta

Grant & Cutler Ltd *in association with*
Tamesis Books Ltd 1983

I.S.B.N. 84-499-6348-6

DEPÓSITO LEGAL: V. 1.847-1983

Printed in Spain by
Artes Gráficas Soler, S.A., Valencia
for
GRANT & CUTLER LTD
11 BUCKINGHAM STREET, LONDON, W.C.2

Contents

For Patricia and Juan Carlos

Prefatory Note

Part of the material of this book was developed for seminars given at the University of Alberta on Alejo Carpentier and the Spanish American Novel. I am grateful to the students who participated in them for their contribution.

El reino de este mundo was first published in Mexico City by Edición y Distribución Iberoamericana de Publicaciones in 1949. Many editions have since appeared and the novel has been translated into several languages. The English translation by Harriet de Onís, titled *The Kingdom of this World*, was first published in New York in 1957 and is currently available in Britain in the Penguin Modern Classics Series. I have used the edition published by the Compañía General de Ediciones (México, 1967), which includes the prologue omitted from some of the later editions, such as that published by the Editorial Seix Barral (Barcelona, 1969). An expanded version of the prologue appeared in Carpentier's volume of essays *Tientos y diferencias* (México: Universidad Nacional Autónoma de México, 1964). An edition of Carpentier's complete works is currently being prepared in Mexico by Siglo XXI Editores.

Italic figures given in parentheses in my text refer to numbered entries in the Bibliographical Note and are followed by a page reference.

1. Introduction

To claim that the appearance of *El reino de este mundo* in 1949 was a significant development for Spanish American literature would be unwarranted. Yet this Cuban novel is one of several works published in the 1940s that have established a place in the history of modern fiction in Spanish. *Ficciones*, by Jorge Luis Borges (Argentina, 1944), *El señor presidente*, by Miguel Angel Asturias (Guatemala, 1946), *Al filo del agua*, by Agustín Yáñez (Mexico, 1947), and *El reino de este mundo* form a group, despite their differences. Their authors shared neither aesthetic principles nor preoccupations, and did not write according to the same techniques. Nonetheless, they do have something in common. The vitality of their writing and sense of innovation contributed to the integration of Spanish American fiction into the mainstream of contemporary literature and demonstrated that Spanish American writers could be more cosmopolitan and, at the same time, more responsive to their own environment. If there is any significance in the date of publication of *El reino de este mundo*, it is therefore that the novel appeared as fiction in Spanish America was emerging from a period of renovation and was beginning to establish a new character.

Regardless of its place in histories of literature, *El reino de este mundo* has an important position among the works of Alejo Carpentier because it is one of his first products of an extended period of searching for new modes of expression. Carpentier associated with the literary avant-garde from his earliest days as a writer. In the 1920s he was a member of the *Grupo minorista* in Cuba and in the 1930s came into close contact with the surrealist movement in Paris. His involvement with some of the more radically progressive forms of artistic expression consequently led him to two inseparable conclusions. He believed that it was necessary for Spanish American writers to respond more effectively to the changing aesthetics of literature and to obtain a better understanding of their continent in order to describe it more fully and accurately. Since he felt that novelists of earlier generations had not fulfilled either of these requirements, he repudiated novels such as *La vorágine*, by José Eustasio Rivera (Colombia, 1924), *Doña Bárbara*, by Rómulo Gallegos (Venezuela, 1929), and even his own first novel *¡Ecué-Yamba-O!* (1933). For him they all gave an erroneously picturesque view of reality based on a response to its external characteristics and too heavily influenced by the outmoded style of nineteenth-century realism. Carpentier's opinion was also fostered by his ability to see America as an outsider. During a period of residence in France (1928-39), he satisfied his curiosity by reading voraciously and interesting himself in the newer forms of expression with which America was then being represented in all the arts. Hence, when he returned to Cuba in 1939 he had a knowledge of the continent and a more finely developed sense of artistic perception that allowed him to discard previous points of view and to see America as if encountering it for the first time. His absence had given him an understanding of reality more mature than that produced solely by a reaction to external circumstances. Above all, he had acquired a feeling for the history of America and an awareness of the complex nature of its relationship with Europe.

The event that led Carpentier from mere speculation on these matters to the composition of a novel was his visit to Haiti in 1943. Contact with the history and culture of that country produced in him the sensation of having discovered a real situation in which all that had concerned him was expressed precisely. By 1949 he had already written several short stories (*Viaje a la semilla*, *Semejante a la noche*, *Los fugitivos*) that indicate the new direction his writing was beginning to take. But it was the publication of *El reino de este mundo* that showed most convincingly the extent to which his ideas had coalesced.

2. History as a Source of Narrative

Carpentier's contention that his predecessors had not portrayed America satisfactorily provokes a legitimate enquiry about how he proposed to remedy their failings. His answer appeared in print in 1964 in an essay entitled 'Problemática de la actual novela latinoamericana'.[1] In that essay he discussed what he termed 'los contextos cabalmente latinoamericanos' and argued that a more faithful representation of reality would be obtained if closer attention were paid to the multiple facets of life (*contextos*) that contribute to the make-up of Latin America and distinguish it from other places. In spite of the fifteen years between publication of *El reino de este mundo* and 'Problemática de la actual novela latinoamericana', there is every reason to link the two. Since a number of the *contextos* had already served as a basis for his fiction, the essay provides the theory for what Carpentier had already practised. Among those relevant to *El reino de este mundo*, for instance, are the conflicting ethnic composition of the continent, the coexistence of primitive and developed cultures, a pattern of political life determined by revolution and violent upheaval, and a boom-or-bust economy dependent on foreign interest. In addition to these similarities, both the essay and *El reino de este mundo* convey a view of Latin America that is based on an understanding of history. The 'contextos cabalmente latinoamericanos' are derived both from events that shaped America and from the circumstances unique to the continent which gave rise to those events and led to the creation of an idiosyncratic society. The authenticity of Carpentier's representation of Latin America in *El reino de este mundo* rests, above all, on his having examined the historical connotations of those same *contextos*. Since the subject-matter of the novel is taken from the history of the continent, it dwells

[1] First published in his *Tientos y diferencias (ensayos)* (México: Universidad Nacional Autónoma de México, 1964), pp.5-46.

on the very process whereby those *contextos* were formed and therefore has a greater claim to being uniquely and authentically Latin American.

In view of the preceding comments, it is hardly surprising that some of the most productive criticism of *El reino de este mundo* has evaluated the role of history in the novel. Such an approach has also been fostered by Carpentier's own statement in the prologue (16) to the first edition that his work was the product of meticulous research. In the light of these circumstances, the precise capacity in which history is a source of the narrative should be clearly established from the outset. It will then be possible to evaluate both the aesthetics of Carpentier's perception of reality and the meaning he intended to convey.

The Chronology of Events

With one exception, the order in which events are narrated in *El reino de este mundo* corresponds exactly to the order of their occurrence in history. Yet, while the reader may be aware of the chronological order of the narrative, he is not necessarily able to determine the period of time that separates one event from the next. Nor is he necessarily able to ascertain at what precise moment in history any given event occurred. Thus, although Carpentier wrote in his prologue that the novel was based on a 'minucioso cotejo de fechas y cronologías' (16), it is not possible to discern what this implies from a reading of the text undertaken without reference to external sources. Many of the incidents described are traceable to specific dates in history, but not a single complete date is cited in the entire novel. It is true that numerous allusions serve the well-informed reader as a guide to the reconstruction of some kind of chronology, but the majority pertain to the largely unfamiliar history of Haiti and many are positively obscure. Moreover, Carpentier has not limited himself to one historical source alone. *El reino de este mundo* is a composite of numerous sources, many of them inaccessible to most readers. The outcome is that much of the novel is esoteric, including the true nature of its chronology. Collation of the incidents narrated in the novel with the events of history from which they are derived will therefore serve several purposes. It will clarify the chronology of the narrative and explain some of the allusions on which it is based. Additionally, it will demonstrate, in part, the nature of the novel as a narrative of historical events.

Part I. The narrative begins at a moment in history that is not specified in the text. References in the first chapter to such events as the arrival of the warship *La Courageuse* at Saint-Domingue (30) are too obscure to be readily dated. However, collation of the incidents related in the early chapters with verifiable historical events is sufficient to establish that the story begins around 1751. In about that year a slave named Mackandal fled the plantation owned by a M. Lenormand (Ch. 3, 'Lo que hallaba la mano'). Mackandal's plot to poison the white population can be placed in the year 1753 (Ch. 5, 'De profundis'). The date may be calculated from the reference in Carpentier's text (57) to Mackandal's four years as a fugitive and from the information in historical sources that he was captured in December 1757, when, as in the novel, he appeared at celebrations on the Defresne plantation (Ch. 7, 'El traje de hombre'). In January or March 1758 — Carpentier describes the occasion as 'un lunes de enero, poco antes del alba' (63) —, Mackandal was executed by burning. Sources differ as to the exact month, just as they differ over the date of the earlier plot. Several historians place both Mackandal's plot and his capture in 1757, thus excluding his four years as a fugitive accounted for in Carpentier's Chapter 6, 'Las metamorfosis'. In any event, the maximum period of time covered in Part I is seven or eight years, the likely dates being 1751-8. It is impossible to deduce such a chronology from the text alone, however. In fact, some indication of how Carpentier refers to time will suffice to illustrate a tendency prevalent throughout the novel. Regardless of references to the four years of Mackandal's absence (57), or to the rainy season (April to September) during which Ti Noel mourned the initial disappearance of Mackandal (44), the duration of events is only vaguely implied. Events occur 'un día' (40, 44, 50), 'una tarde' (48), or 'cierta tarde' (50), with little indication of the interval between them. The closest to an exact date is the information concerning Mackandal's execution (quoted above) or the reference to the death of Lenormand's first wife: 'Madame Lenormand de Mezy falleció el domingo de Pentecostés, poco después de probar una naranja particularmente hermosa que una rama, demasiado complaciente, había puesto al alcance de sus manos' (49-50). Although Carpentier has evidently followed a sequence of historical events, he has just as evidently paid no attention to establishing their precise chronology for the reader to see. In this light, it is perhaps less important for us to know that Part I ends on a Monday in January in 1758 than to have realized that Ti Noel begins the novel as a boy ('el mozo', 33 and 43) who has certainly proven his manhood by the end of Part I.

Part II. The second part of the novel covers a longer period of time than Part I. Its first chapter, 'La hija de Minos y de Pasifae', is intended to bridge thirty-three years between the execution of Mackandal in 1758 and the slave rebellion led by Bouckman in 1791. In general, it reflects the economic prosperity and moral decadence of Saint-Domingue in the second half of the eighteenth century. The title of the chapter is therefore suitably ironic. It refers to the actress wife of M. Lenormand, who drunkenly recites (75-6) the role of Phaedra (Daughter of Minos and Pasiphae) from the play by the French classical dramatist Jean Racine. The passage of time is clearly evident in the text through references to the life of M. Lenormand. Ti Noel's visit to Cap Français (Cabo Francés), described at the beginning of the chapter, occurs after the death of Lenormand's second wife. As the narrative proceeds, it is learned that after a brief, intemperate life as a widower Lenormand went to France, married Mlle Floridor, and returned with her to Saint-Domingue. The last part of the chapter then contains a description of life in Lenormand's household twenty years later. This sequence of events is sufficient to give the reader the impression that a considerable period of time has elapsed since the end of Part I of the novel, but it is worth noting that the exact duration of this period is obscured.

Ti Noel's visit to Cap Français, related in the first paragraph of the chapter, provides the pretext for a description (71-2) of the progress of the city. Since the first part of the novel also

begins with a visit to Cap Français by Ti Noel, the reader is implicitly invited to compare the two occasions and is made aware
that a significant period of time has elapsed between them.
Moreover, a number of references to specific historical circumstances make it possible to arrive at an approximate date for
Ti Noel's later visit. The *Gazette de Saint Domingue* (71) began
publication in 1764, the same year in which a theatre opened on
the Rue Vaudreuil (71-2). L'Auberge de la Couronne (La
Corona in the text, 72), was the name of an inn on the Rue
Espagnole jointly owned by a Mlle Mongeon and a sugar planter
named M. Bâdeche. It had won considerable celebrity by about
1787 after it was bought by Henri Christophe, the future king of
Northern Haiti. With the notable exception of the dates, most of
these details appear in the text, thereby permitting the conclusion that Ti Noel must have visited the city after 1787.

Following the description of Cap Français, the narrative is
renewed in the next paragraph with an acccount (72-4) of
Lenormand's life since the death of his second wife, including
the few months he spent in France and his third marriage.
Although the sequence of events is clear, the statement at the
beginning of the third paragraph, 'Sobre todo esto habían
transcurrido veinte años' (74), makes it difficult to establish a
clear chronology. The statement implies that twenty years have
elapsed since Ti Noel's visit to Cap Français described at the
beginning of the chapter. Since the reference to Christophe's
ownership of La Corona places that visit not much earlier than
1787, the description of life in Lenormand's household in the
final paragraphs of the chapter, including Lenormand's
'erotomanía' (74) and Mlle Floridor's drunken recitations,
would have to belong to the years 1807 and after. As the
chronology of the remainder of the novel reveals, however, this
is not possible because Lenormand left Saint-Domingue for
Cuba long before that date. Another possible explanation is that
the period of twenty years refers to the time elapsed since the end
of the previous chapter. But, while 1807 is too late, 1778, twenty
years after Mackandal's execution, is clearly too early. Undoubtedly what Carpentier intended in this chapter was to convey the impression that a lengthy period of time had passed and

to give some indication of what had occurred in the interval, but the way he has done so does not enhance his claim that *El reino de este mundo* is the product of a 'minucioso cotejo de fechas y cronologías'.

The events narrated in the second and third chapters of Part II can, by contrast, be attributed to very precise dates. The Voodoo conspiracy led by Bouckman (Ch. 2, 'El Pacto Mayor') took place on the night of Sunday, 14 August 1791. The call to rebellion (Ch. 3, 'La llamada de los caracoles') came eight days later (80) on the night of 22 August 1791. Both dates are confirmed by all historical sources. The fourth chapter, 'Dogón dento del arca', covers the next few days. After the uprising, Lenormand spent two days hiding in a well (87) and several days in his house (88) before hearing of Bouckman's capture and then going to Cap Français. Thus far, the narrative is perfectly synchronized with history since Bouckman was taken in the early days of the rebellion. However, the chronology is less easy to follow at the end of the chapter. When Lenormand reaches Cap Français he finds the city in confusion and, apparently on the same day, arranges for a passage to Cuba. Although the vessel on which he is due to sail had been delayed for several months (because of the rebellion?), it nonetheless seems all but ready to leave. The overall impression, therefore, is that Lenormand sailed for Cuba soon after the uprising, perhaps in late August or early September 1791. On arrival in Santiago, as described at the beginning of the next chapter (93), he encounters numerous refugees who had preceded him. It is a little surprising to learn that they are already well established in their new surroundings and have even erected a theatre (94). Evidently the lapse of time between the end of the fourth chapter and the beginning of the fifth must be greater than is immediately apparent.

The description of Lenormand's life in Santiago de Cuba contained in the fifth chapter entails a maximum of twelve years. It may be assumed, as has been seen, that he arrived in 1791. By the end of the chapter, no later than 1803, he has begun to feel his age and a sense of remorse for his dissipated life. The second date is confirmed by references to Esteban Salas and to the dogs sent to Saint-Domingue which are mentioned at the beginning of the next chapter. Salas, a Cuban composer and Chapel Master of the Cathedral in Santiago de Cuba, was buried on 15 July 1803. When Lenormand and Ti Noel went into the Cathedral and saw Salas rehearsing the choir (97-8) it must therefore have been before that date. It would have been precisely in 1803, however, that Ti Noel saw 'la nave de los perros'. The dogs are referred to twice, at the beginning of the sixth (101) and at the end of the seventh chapters (115). On the second occasion it is learned that they were used by Governor Rochambeau in his campaign against the negroes in Saint-Domingue, an allusion to the year 1803. Between the two references, however, there is a deliberate disruption of the chronology. On the same day that Ti Noel saw the dogs put on board ship he also heard news brought by recent refugees from Saint-Domingue (102). What he heard, in effect, was an account of the French invasion, an episode narrated in Chapters 6 and 7 by means of a flashback and from the point of view of the experiences of Napoleon's sister, Pauline Bonaparte.

The armada that carried Pauline and the French expeditionary force under the command of her husband, General Leclerc, sailed from Brest on 14 December 1801, and reached its destination on 29 January 1802. Leclerc's campaign was adversely affected by yellow fever and he died of the disease on 2 November 1802. His command passed to Rochambeau and his widow returned with his body to France. These events are all reflected in the novel, but a number of changes have been introduced into the account of Pauline's experiences. History confirms that she travelled on the flagship Océan (102) and delayed the departure of the entire armada for almost two months while she shopped in Paris and then journeyed at a painfully slow pace to Brest (103). However, the first part of her journey was not destined to make her feel like a queen (102). She was a very reluctant passenger. The weather was atrocious and she was positively miserable. Arriving in Saint-Domingue, she spent the first few months at Port-au-Prince in the South, not at Cap Français on the Northern Plain (105). Only then did she go to Tortuga, the island off the northern coast of Haiti. She later returned to Cap Français and took up residence at Government House in the city. It was there that she remained till her departure for France and there that her husband died, not in Tortuga, as indicated in the text.

Part III. It is clear from the very beginning of the first chapter that a period of several years has gone by since the end of Part II. Ti Noel is an old man when he returns home from Cuba ('un negro, viejo pero firme aún sobre sus pies juanetudos y escamados', 119). Lenormand has been dead for several years. Ti Noel is free and believes that slavery has been abolished in Haiti. The passage of time is also evident from other changes. The land has been abandoned and is overgrown, and the regime, different from the one Ti Noel had known before, has a number of surprises in store for him. The text, however, contains no immediate indication of the number of years that have passed in the interval between the second and third parts of the novel.

The failure of the French to recapture their colony was followed soon after by the declaration of Haitian independence in January 1804. The assassination of the first president, later emperor, Jean-Jacques Dessalines, in 1806 led to the division of Haiti into two states. From 1807, the North was ruled by Henri Christophe, who proclaimed himself king in 1811. Sans-Souci, his favourite palace at Millot, was completed in 1813 and his citadel at La Ferrière was still incomplete at the end of his reign. Although it seems a little early, several sources give 1804 as the year in which work on the citadel began. Since it had already been under construction for more than twelve years (134) before Ti Noel was conscripted into the labour gang, he must have returned to Haiti in about 1816. The date fits in well with the events that follow. The earliest date given in sources for the death of Corneille Breille (Cornejo Breille in the text) described in Chapter 4, 'El emparedado', is 1816. The latest is shortly before 15 August 1820, which Carpentier has apparently accepted. This date allows for the fact that Ti Noel spent almost a year among the ruins of Lenormand's estate (140-1) before he witnessed Breille's death agony during a visit to Cap Français and that, prior to that incident, he spent an unspecified period on the construction of the citadel. It also maintains the historical continuity of the novel, since the chapter immediately after the account of Breille's death is entitled 'La crónica del 15 de agosto' and deals with events of 1820. However, regardless of his attention to chronology, Carpentier obscures the true length of Ti Noel's stay in Cuba. As we shall see later, he tends to convey the impression that certain periods of time were shorter than they really were.

The final three chapters of Part III have few immediate problems. On 15 August 1820, the feast of the Assumption, Henri Christophe attended mass at the parish church of Limonade to celebrate the fête of his queen Marie-Louise. During the service, conducted by Archbishop González, he suffered a stroke (Ch. 5, 'La crónica del 15 de agosto'). The outcome is accurately narrated in the following chapters (Ch. 6, 'Ultima ratio regum', and Ch. 7, 'La única puerta'). Confronted by a general rebellion sparked by an army mutiny, Christophe proved to be physically incapable of retaining control of his kingdom and committed suicide. Accompanied by his wife and two daughters, his body was carried by a few loyal subjects to La Ferrière, where it was buried in quicklime originally intended for use in the construction of the citadel. One date appears to have been changed. The reference to 'El domingo siguiente a la puesta del sol...' (153) at the beginning of the sixth chapter insinuates that the rebellion and Christophe's death occurred no later than a week after he suffered a stroke. In reality, he died on Sunday, 8 October 1820.

Part IV. As at the beginning of the second and third parts of the novel, the narrative is resumed in the final part after an interval of an unspecified number of years. The survivors of Christophe's family, his wife, Marie-Louise, and his daughters, Atenais and Amatista, are in Italy (Ch. 1, 'La noche de las estatuas'). Ti Noel has aged still further and, in this part of the novel, is consistently referred to as 'el anciano' (181, 182, 184, 189, etc.). Moreover, he witnesses further changes in the political status of Haiti. The period of time in question, however, can be ascertained only by reference to external sources. Marie-Louise and her daughters arrived in Italy in September 1824, and settled in Pisa (not Rome, as in the text). Since they had been in England prior to that date, the statement that 'las princesas conocían, por primera vez en Europa, un

verano que les supiera a verano' (171) places the time in the summer of 1825. This date is also compatible with Solimán's
discovery of the statue of Pauline Bonaparte in the Borghese
Palace in Rome, an incident which clarifies why Carpentier ignored his sources and did not make Pisa the city where
Christophe's family settled in Italy. After her return to France,
Pauline married into the Borghese family, and the statue of her
as 'Venus Victrix' referred to in the text was completed by the
Italian sculptor Antonio Canova (1752-1822) in about 1807. The
description of the statue as 'el cadáver de Pauline Bonaparte'
(178) and the impression that the Borghese Palace is like an empty mausoleum (174-6) tend to confirm the date as 1825, the year
in which Pauline died.

By 1825, Haiti had been reunited under the presidency of the
mulatto Jean-Pierre Boyer. Among his legislative endeavours
was the promulgation on 1 May 1826 of a *Code Rural* implementing a series of measures designed to restore the countryside and
return the land to agriculture. The surveyors ('los agrimensores')
encountered by Ti Noel would therefore have appeared in Northern Haiti some time after 1826. A brief reference (189) to a
visit to the spa at Carlsbad by Marie-Louise and her daughters
places the event in 1830. Finally, the apocalyptic ending of the
novel, with references to destruction by fire (197) and the sea
(198), appears to combine disasters which struck Southern Haiti
in the following two years but which Carpentier has located in
the North. On the night of 12-13 August 1831, the port of Les
Cayes was struck by a hurricane and tidal wave, and in July
1832, sections of Port-au-Prince were destroyed by fire. Another
possibility is that the end of the novel refers to the earthquake of
7 May 1842, which affected the entire island of Hispaniola and
killed 10,000 persons in Cap Haitien, the name given to Cap
Français since independence. As we shall see, however, this
possibility would extend the duration of time in the novel
beyond the limits of what can be reasonably expected.

In the preceding collation of the incidents narrated in *El reino
de este mundo* with the events of history no attempt has been
made to distinguish between fact and fiction. The chronology
established, however, is sufficient to demonstrate that history is

not simply background material, but is the subject of the narrative and has, for the most part, been meticulously observed by Carpentier. In summary, the central incident in each of the four parts of the novel is derived from one of four significant episodes in the history of Haiti. The colonial era is represented by Mackandal's conspiracy in the 1750s (Part I) and by the slave rebellion led by Bouckman in 1791 (Part II). The post-colonial period is portrayed through the downfall of Henri Christophe in 1820 (Part III) and through the subsequent re-establishment of republican government (Part IV). Moreover, the hiatus between those two periods is bridged by a narrative (in Part II) which, although not directly centred on the political history of Haiti, nonetheless reflects the collapse of colonial society and the war of independence. By basing himself on those four episodes, Carpentier committed himself to the narration of a relatively specific period of time, a period of approximately eighty years from about 1751 to about 1830-2. Although it is difficult to arrive at that figure without reference to external sources, Carpentier has provided a mechanism that at least allows the reader to obtain some notion of the total period of time involved. He wrote in his prologue that *El reino de este mundo* is based on a succession of extraordinary events 'que no alcanza el lapso de una vida humana' (16). The lives of Lenormand and Ti Noel therefore serve an important function in relation to the chronology of the novel. But there are some problems. The span of eighty years encompassed by the narrative is not shorter but longer than a normal human life. Moreover, when considered in the light of the chronology established for the novel, the lives of both Ti Noel and Lenormand exceed reasonable expectations.

The life of Ti Noel spans the entire novel, and since he was at least an adolescent at its beginning it is reasonable to suppose that he was over ninety by its end. Such an advanced age is not, of course, impossible. But it is a rather remarkable feat of survival at a time when the life expectancy of the negro was barely thirty-five years. It is impossible to calculate the exact year of Lenormand's death. When Ti Noel returned to Haiti from Cuba, his former master had been dead for several years (119). He was certainly still alive, however, when the two of them heard Esteban Salas at work in Santiago Cathedral (97). A possible date for Lenormand's death could therefore be about 1803, the year that Salas died. Since the novel begins in about 1751, it may consequently be assumed that its first two parts trace approximately the last fifty years of Lenormand's life. By the beginning of the novel, however, Lenormand has already contracted his first of three marriages and has attained the status of a wealthy landowner. It must be concluded, as a result, that he was well over seventy by the time of his death. Such an age is quite an accomplishment for one who led so dissipated an existence. The essential problem, as in the case of Ti Noel, is that it calls the verisimilitude of the novel into question. But, in the light of this observation, it is appropriate to return to one of the characteristics of the chronology mentioned earlier.

Although thirty-three years elapsed between the execution of Mackandal in 1758 and the rebellion led by Bouckman in 1791, the only specific guide given to the reader is a reference to the passage of twenty years in the life of Lenormand and his household (74). Similarly, the only guide that the reader has for the duration of Ti Noel's absence from Haiti is the reference to the twelve years during which the citadel at La Ferrière had been under construction before he began to work there (134). In reality, he must have been in Cuba for at least twenty-five years between 1791 and 1816. These two instances, however, should not be taken in isolation. They should be combined with the fact that specific dates are lacking throughout the text, that the duration of events is not always clearly established, and that the period of time from one event to the next is not easily verified from the text alone. The compound effect of all these factors is to create the impression that the time which passes in the novel is, in fact, shorter than the time which passed in history. The reader is deluded into accepting that all the events narrated in the novel could easily have occurred within the span of a single lifetime. If this is the case, then Carpentier's claim to have written a novel founded on a 'minucioso cotejo de fechas y cronologías' acquires a certain duplicity. On the one hand, his statement may be taken as an affirmation of the relationship between the novel and history. This is the sense in which it is usually taken, and collation of the narrative with history generally confirms it. On the other hand, in view of the discrepancies in chronology that have been uncovered, his claim is not entirely true. Yet there is an element of truth in it which pertains only to the work as a novel free of the limitations of history. In this context, the meticulous collation of dates and chronologies spoken of by Carpentier may equally be taken as a reference to the manner in which he has endeavoured to preserve the verisimilitude of his own narrative. That is to say that, without perceptibly disrupting the chronology of history, he has altered it sufficiently to adjust it to the demands of fiction. The collation of incidents narrated in the novel with the events of history therefore reveals one of the important bases of Carpentier's art as a novelist. It demonstrates that when departing, however marginally, from the chronology of history, he has remoulded it in such a way that he is still able to remain faithful to the reality he wished to portray.

Fact and Fiction

In his portrayal of the principal historical figures and events, Carpentier has adhered strictly to his sources. Relatively little is known about Mackandal. He was brought to Saint-Domingue from West Africa as a slave and was owned by a M. Lenormand de Mezy. Maimed in an accident and incapacitated for manual labour, he was assigned to tend cattle. He escaped, became a leader among the maroons (fugitive slaves), and, after an unsuccessful attempt to poison the white population, was eventually captured, tried, and executed by burning. These few facts represent a consensus of what Carpentier could have gleaned from his reading and he has not significantly departed from it in his novel. He has even retained many of the accompanying details, such as the circumstances of Mackandal's capture on the Dufresne plantation, and has elaborated his character in accordance with historical documentation. In addition to government papers of the period and the work of more recent historians, Carpentier also read the diaries, correspondence, and accounts written in the eighteenth century by inhabitants of Saint-Domingue and by visitors to the colony. Among the most significant was the work of Moreau de Saint-Mery, who is referred to in the novel (91), and whose monumental *Description topographique, physique, civile, politique et historique de la partie française de l'Isle de Saint-Domingue* was published in three volumes in Philadelphia, 1797-8. Thus, when Carpentier described the effects of Mackandal's plot he knew that his very name had become synonymous with the poison frequently used by the slaves in colonial times and that the plantation owners and their families lived in perpetual fear of their lives. He was equally aware of the personality attributed to Mackandal. Historians describe him as a seductive, charismatic figure, who had attained the status of a prophet among his followers. His powers of metamorphosis derived from the Voodoo belief in animism and the story of his escape from the fire to which he was condemned was reported by Moreau de Saint-Mery. Evidently, as in Carpentier's novel, the figure of Mackandal had already entered the realm of legend before the end of the eighteenth century.

The account of Bouckman's conspiracy is a similar product of historical sources. The earliest version of it is preserved in the French Colonial Archives in the form of a report of confessions extracted from participants published in 1792 for the French National Assembly. The essential details coincide exactly with what is contained in the novel. The conspirators met in the Bois Caimán on the Northern Plain of Haiti in the midst of the torrential rain of a tropical thunderstorm. After a Voodoo ceremony, which included the ritual slaughter of a pig and the tasting of its blood, a plan of rebellion was formulated. Bouckman's address to the slaves, reported in the novel, is an exact transcription of what, according to the sources, was spoken in Creole. Carpentier's limitation of the episode to a single brief chapter is itself an indication of his respect for his sources. Since history has preserved little else about the conspiracy, any further elaboration would have depended entirely on Carpentier's own invention. With the exception of the presence of Ti Noel at the scene, he has in fact refrained from any noteworthy development.

The general accuracy with which the downfall of Henri

Christophe is narrated has already been sufficiently demonstrated through discussion of its chronology. It must be added, however, that the faithfulness to detail which accompanies the portrayal of Mackandal and Bouckman is equally evident in the part of the novel that pertains to Christophe. The atmosphere evoked by the description of his regime, his palace at Millot, the building of his citadel, and his actual downfall is obtained in part through the accumulation of innumerable details taken from history and popular tradition. In the account of Christophe's last days, for instance, references to the silencing of the animals for fear of disturbing the king (150), to the princesses' American governess (151), to the desertion of the palace guard (155), and even to the finger severed from Christophe's hand after his death (167), can all be readily substantiated. As has been aptly stated, although with regard to other references, 'Examples such as these could be multiplied until the entire text of the story, or very nearly, could be set against some historical text' (*8*, p.135).

The preceding comments show that Carpentier has had recourse to history to a very remarkable extent for the composition of *El reino de este mundo*. He has not just narrated a series of historical events, but has consolidated his account with detailed accuracy. His ability to incorporate countless minute and historically accurate details into his text is the evident product of particular circumstances. Shortly after his visit to Haiti in 1943 he was commissioned by the Mexican publishing house Fondo de Cultura Económica to write *La música en Cuba*. The research undertaken for that project gave a depth to his knowledge of Caribbean history that went far beyond his curiosity about America in the 1930s and also exceeded his immediate needs as a musicologist. At the same time, his acquisition of an intimate knowledge of history fruitfully coincided with his own response to the uniqueness of Latin America that he experienced after his return to Cuba from France in 1939 and as a consequence of his visit to Haiti in 1943. The bibliography appended to *La música en Cuba* is an excellent guide to materials read by Carpentier shortly before writing *El reino de este mundo* and contains several items indispensable for the verification of its historical bases. Indeed, *La música en Cuba* is itself a useful source-book.

Carpentier's two works inevitably coincide most in their accounts of the effects on Cuban society produced by the refugees who fled from Saint-Domingue after the slave rebellion of 1791. The description of Lenormand's life in exile, contained in the chapter entitled 'Santiago de Cuba' in Part II of the novel, has a significant precedent in Carpentier's work in the first few pages of Chapter 6 of *La música en Cuba*, 'Introducción de la contradanza' (*4*, pp.121-30). In addition to a summary of the history of Saint-Domingue, those pages contain many of the details that appear in the novel. It is confirmed, for instance, that many refugees escaped in much the same way as Lenormand on whatever vessel would carry them and with whatever possessions could be salvaged. The musician from Alsace who is described in the novel (93) as having salvaged his clavichord and sailed with Lenormand is perhaps the same Karl Rischer who is mentioned in *La música en Cuba* (*4*, p.128) as the co-founder of an orchestra. Those who were more fortunate re-established in Cuba the style of life they had enjoyed in Saint-Domingue, or were able to find passage to New Orleans in Louisiana, which was to remain a French colony until 1803. As is described in both *La música en Cuba* and *El reino de este mundo*, however, the refugees who remained in Cuba significantly gallicized Cuban society. Those who could exploited their talents as teachers of French, music, or dancing, and created an increasing demand for French culture. The theatre encountered by Lenormand on his arrival in Santiago was erected by the first refugees. The introduction of fashionable European dances, particularly the *contredanse*, revitalized popular music in Cuba. Evidently the former colonists of Saint-Domingue had abandoned their colony but not their culture. Like Lenormand in *El reino de este mundo*, they endeavoured to preserve the familiar customs of earlier and happier days. Thus, the practice reported in the novel (96-7) of rising for both the republican *Marseillaise* and the monarchist *Hymne de Saint Louis* at the close of an evening's entertainment, far from apocryphal, is corroborated in *La música en Cuba* (*4*, p.128).

Aside from giving rise to the phenomenon of a novelist who

has written his own historical source, the existence of *La música en Cuba* is a further indication of the extent of Carpentier's use of history in *El reino de este mundo*. It not only demonstrates that Carpentier considered the same material as pertinent to both a work of history and the composition of a work of fiction, but stresses the relationship in his own mind between the two genres. Yet, in spite of the clearly factual basis of much of the novel, Carpentier's narrative is evidently not entirely historical. It lacks a totally objective point of view and has certain characteristics that would be unacceptable in a purely historical account. As has already been established, the chronology of events is subjected to some manipulation. Extended periods of time are omitted from the narrative; precise dates and sufficient indication of the duration of episodes are also lacking. In reality, *El reino de este mundo* must be seen as the product of a particular kind of interaction between fact and fiction. While there is no radical departure from source materials, history is nonetheless presented from the perspective of fiction and is subject to a structure and interpretation imposed upon it by the novelist. The nature of this kind of transformation will be discussed more fully in a commentary on the meaning of the novel as a whole. For the moment, it need only be shown how the novel is a product of the combination of history and fiction.

As has been demonstrated, both the principal incidents of the novel and the characters central to them, Mackandal, Bouckman, and Christophe, are portrayed with an almost absolute respect for historical accuracy. By contrast, Lenormand, Ti Noel, and Solimán, the three characters whose lives serve as a means of connecting the incidents and establishing narrative continuity, are principally fictional. The life of Lenormand de Mezy, for instance, plays an important role in the first two parts of the novel as one of the focal points of the narrative. He is to be identified with a figure of the same name referred to by Moreau de Saint-Mery as the owner of property in Le Limbé and Le Morne Rouge in the northern part of Saint-Domingue, the very estates from which Mackandal escaped. The identification cannot be taken any further, however. Carpentier's Lenormand is principally his own creation. He is perhaps a composite of

characteristics derived from many historical figures encountered
by Carpentier in his reading, but represents a particular social
class rather than a single individual from history. Ti Noel is
related to a variety of sources. In a play by the Haitian writer
Isnardin Vieux (1865-1941) entitled *Mackandal* (1925) there is a
slave called Ti Noel who is owned by Lenormand de Mezy and is
a faithful follower of Mackandal. Two historical figures also
have the same name. A slave named Noël was the leader of a
minor uprising in the early part of the eighteenth century and
Petit-Noël Prière was the name of a rebel leader and rival of
Henri Christophe at the time of the war against the French
(1802-3). This may have been enough to suggest the use of Ti
Noel as an appropriate name for the character intended to represent the slave population as a whole. But the name itself is as
common as John or Joseph and is more important in the novel
for symbolic than for historical overtones. The characterization
of Ti Noel must therefore be considered as deriving from
Carpentier's general familiarity with the life of the negro in the
period with which he is concerned. Finally, there is Solimán,
whose role as a source of continuity in the second half of the
novel has frequently been overlooked by commentators. A person named Solimán is mentioned in one source as a retainer in
Christophe's court who accompanied the royal family into exile
in Italy. The association between Solimán and Pauline
Bonaparte, however, was invented by Carpentier.

Although these three characters are all predominantly fictional, their lives are narrated as if they were historical.
Moreover, it is not just a matter of Carpentier's having
associated them with or involved them in the historical dramas
central to the novel. Throughout *El reino de este mundo* their
character and conduct are described in the terms of the historical
context of the period to which they are made to belong. Comparison with *La música en Cuba*, for instance, has revealed that
had a person such as Lenormand sought refuge in Cuba from
the turmoil in Saint-Domingue he would have encountered exactly the circumstances described in the novel and would have
lived out his life there much as Carpentier narrated it. In effect,
it is precisely this and similar situations which give rise to the

particular kind of interaction between history and fiction referred to earlier. What it amounts to is that just as fiction provides the pretext for the narration of history, so history itself lends an air of authenticity to fiction. The process may be more properly documented through analysis of 'La llamada de los caracoles', the third chapter of Part II of the novel.

The outbreak of the slave rebellion of 1791 is represented in 'La llamada de los caracoles' through a description of incidents occurring on Lenormand's estate. Since they were not derived from a documented life of the character, Lenormand's feelings of pessimism and his hiding behind a clump of bougainvillea to escape the rebels must be attributed to Carpentier's invention. The same is true of the subsequent pillaging of his house and the massacre of its inhabitants. That is to say that the historical uprising is represented by an essentially fictional account. At the same time, however, this account is authenticated to an extent that makes it acceptable as history. In the first instance, there is a basis in history for the existence of Lenormand. In the second, the rebellion is known to have erupted in much the same way as described. But, above all, the events narrated in the chapter are located within a context elaborated from very precise historical details.

Although fictional, Lenormand's pessimism can be traced to real historical circumstances. It purports to derive from a conversation he had with the Governor of Saint-Domingue, a report of which occupies the greater part of the first paragraph of the chapter. Regardless of any irony implicit in the meaning of his name, Blanchelande was, in reality, the Chief Administrator of Saint-Domingue in 1791. His views are narrated in the text in indirect free speech,[2] a form which, combined with the authenticity of his identity, creates a heightened sense of actuality. Moreover, the opinions attributed to him are a fairly succinct summary of prevailing contemporary attitudes. The colonists of Saint-Domingue were opposed to reform. They were prepared to withstand recent racial disturbances and, like Blanchelande, scoffed at the resolution passed by the National Assembly in

---

[2] Use of this form in *El reino de este mundo* is discussed in more detail in Chapter 5, below.

Paris (May 1791) whereby political rights were granted to mulattoes. Blancheland's opinion that the revolutionary government in France had been infected by liberalism and was prepared to stand on principles derived from an erroneously idyllic view of the colonies is consequently endorsed by the conduct of political life in Saint-Domingue. Moreover, his opinion is substantiated by a series of predominantly pejorative references to eighteenth-century figures noted for their idealized depiction of reality. Thus Abraham Brunias was the name incorrectly given to the engraver Augustin Brunais whose romanticized scenes of Saint-Domingue, including the slave market, were exhibited in London by the Royal Academy in 1777 and 1779. The Vicomte de Parny was a minor French poet from the Indian Ocean colony of Saint Paul who celebrated colonial life in his verses. 'El vicario saboyano' was, of course, Jean-Jacques Rousseau, one of whose meeting places was the Café de la Régence in Paris. 'El paraíso vegetal de Pablo y Virginia' is a reference to the immensely popular sentimental novel by Bernardin de Saint Pierre which, as Carpentier's own description of Pauline Bonaparte reveals only too readily, did much to foster misconceptions about the colonies. Finally, Estanislao de Wimpffen was a contemporary observer of life in Saint-Domingue, who visited the colony between 1788 and 1790 and whose correspondence was published in French and English editions in 1797.

The accumulation of so much historical detail in the same paragraph has a significant effect. Since Lenormand's fears are expressed in terms of a reaction to an historically authentic view of colonial life, the description of his anxiety results in the elaboration of the precise historical context in which his preoccupations are to be understood. This context, in turn, then provides the very basis for accepting Lenormand's state of mind as a genuine reflection of reality. In addition, it creates the context in which to place the events narrated in the latter part of the chapter. Thus Lenormand's sombre meditations are interrupted by a realization of the worst of the fears he had received from Blanchelande. He is confronted with the very slave rebellion predicted by the Governor and expected by the reader since the preceding chapter ('El Pacto Major'), in which Bouckman's conspiracy had been described with remarkable fidelity to historical sources. The presumed fictional portions of 'La llamada de los caracoles' are therefore so enmeshed in historical data and incident that history and fiction are perfectly integrated.

The process evident in 'La llamada de los caracoles' occurs throughout the novel and has the effect of establishing all that is narrated as a proper representation of history. There are, for example, a number of incidents, fictional and non-fictional, that might well be regarded as fantastically extravagant. Yet all of them can be explained or authenticated in the light of some historical source. There is ample precedent for Lenormand's extravagantly dissipated existence; a belief in Mackandal's metamorphosis and final escape is documented; and the ruins of Christophe's citadel and of the palace of Sans-Souci at Millot are still standing. Three instances require particular commentary. The metamorphosis and disappearance of Ti Noel at the end of the novel and Solimán's reaction to the statue he discovers in Rome will be dealt with later, but the introduction of Pauline Bonaparte is worthy of immediate comment. Since she was the wife of General Leclerc and was in fact commanded by her brother, Napoleon, to accompany her husband to Saint-Domingue, her inclusion in the novel is entirely legitimate. But the account of her sojourn in the Caribbean is characterized by several aspects that distinguish it from other episodes in the novel. In the first instance, it is presented in the context of a flashback and is, as noted earlier, the only episode which disrupts the linear chronology of the narrative. Secondly, it not only contains several changes to the historical sources, but shifts the focus of the narrative away from the political history of Haiti and onto incidents historically more marginal. Above all, Carpentier has introduced the episode relating to Pauline and Solimán, a development which is entirely fictional and is therefore significantly unusual because the life of Pauline Bonaparte is appropriately documented in the sources. The meaning of the entire episode, including the resonances it produces in the final part of the novel when Solimán appears in Rome in the entourage of Christophe's widow, will be dealt with later during discussion of interpretations of the novel as a whole. For the moment it is relevant only to establish on what basis Carpentier has developed the fictional elements of Pauline's character.

From among the sources on which Carpentier could have relied for a portrait of Pauline Bonaparte, he has drawn from the memoirs of Mme Laure Junot, Duchesse d'Abrantès. A passage from her anecdotal account of life in France under Napoleon is quoted as the epigraph to Part II of *El reino de este mundo* and she is referred to in the text (103) as Pauline's advisor in matters of fashion. Notwithstanding the suspicion with which historians regard them, Mme Junot's memoirs have the distinct advantage for the novelist of not being limited to the purely factual. Thus, while they contain an accurate account of preparations for the expedition to Saint-Domingue, which confirms a number of details found in the novel, they also convey Mme Junot's personal evaluation of Pauline's reaction to the whole affair. Pauline emerges as a notoriously capricious woman, readily possessed of the most extravagant notions and just as ready to abandon them in favour of others equally extravagant. As Mme Junot writes, 'She was, for example, certainly nothing less than naïve, and yet every day she managed to say and do things that a young girl, a child would not have imagined.'[3] On the basis of this assessment, confirmed, incidentally, by other sources, Carpentier's depiction of Pauline acquires a distinct air of reality. However extravagant, it is credible for her to have seen herself as a character from a novel living in an island paradise, and just as credible for her to have had recourse to Solimán's Voodoo remedies when her paradise was disrupted by yellow fever. By the same token, it is not in the least remarkable that, as she sailed home for France, her role as the grieving widow did not prevent her from forming a liaison with the officer assigned to guard her husband's coffin. The portrayal of Pauline Bonaparte is consequently characterized by the

---

[3] 'Elle n'était, par exemple, riens moins que naïve assurément, et pourtant il lui arrivait chaque jour de dire, de faire des choses qu'une jeune fille, une enfant n'aurait pas imaginé' (Laure Junot, Duchesse d'Abrantès, *Mémoires de la duchesse d'Abrantès: souvenirs historiques sur le Consulat*, with an introduction by G. Girard, Paris: A la Cité des Livres, 1930, IV, p.54).

same kind of integration between history and fiction that is evident in the creation of Lenormand.

It is largely on account of the relationship between history and fiction that *El reino de este mundo* differs from conventional historical novels. In the conventional historical novel, such as that patterned after the work of Sir Walter Scott, history is not necessarily related for its own sake. It is generally exploited as background and used to create a setting in which to locate a predominantly fictional narrative. By contrast, Carpentier's novel is the product of a different and more complex process. History itself is the basis of the narrative of *El reino de este mundo* and matters of both fact and fiction are told with such attention to accuracy that some of the minutest details of description can be verified in the appropriate sources. It would require an extensively annotated edition of the novel to document them all. The basis of Carpentier's method of composition, therefore, is not that he exploits history in order to produce fiction, but rather that his fiction is written as if it were history. The elaborations of Lenormand de Mezy and Pauline Bonaparte are excellent cases in point. Regardless of the little that is known about Lenormand and the little that was appropriate for Carpentier's purposes, he nonetheless emerges in the novel as a fully documented character. The sense of history that surrounds him is as complete as that surrounding Henri Christophe. This is precisely the effect that Carpentier needed to obtain. If he was to write fiction and yet convey the contexts of history to their fullest extent, he necessarily had to limit any sense of demarcation between the two. Fiction and history had to be written not so much as if they were one and the same but so that they would appear to be the same. This is not to say that they should have the same formal characteristics of composition, but that they should derive from a common perception of reality and therefore admit a common interpretation. The importance of establishing this fact and of fully understanding the extent and manner of Carpentier's use of history in *El reino de este mundo* will become increasingly evident in the following chapters when some consideration of his sense of aesthetics and his interpretation of reality is undertaken.

3. 'Lo real maravilloso americano'

Carpentier's preoccupation with the coalescence of history and fiction is reflected in a comment about one of his more recent novels, *El recurso del método* (1974): 'Yo soy absolutamente incapaz de "inventar" una historia. Todo lo que escribo es "montaje" de cosas vividas, observadas, recordadas, y agrupadas, luego, en un cuerpo coherente.'[4] Since we have already shown that his recourse to history does not entirely exclude the possibility of invention, his statement should evidently not be taken too literally. The way in which fact and fiction are integrated in *El reino de este mundo*, however, is a guide to the limits Carpentier imposed on the exercise of his imagination and an indication of the circumstances that motivated his comment about *El recurso del método*. As we shall see, his comment may be correctly interpreted as an emphatic assertion of his conviction that imagination should be subordinated to reality.

Several critics have traced the development of Carpentier's thought during the early part of his career as a writer. Adolfo Cruz-Luis (*14*) has examined articles written between 1923 and 1949 for *Social* (Havana), *Carteles* (Havana), and *El Nacional* (Caracas), and shown that Carpentier's evaluation of the culture and history of Latin America underwent a significant evolution during a period of more than twenty years before the publication of *El reino de este mundo*. His point of view was profoundly influenced by his reaction to the portrayal of America in art and literature, by a prolonged absence from Cuba (1928-39), and by his own interpretation of America derived from observation and a reading of history. Studies by Emil Volek (*25*), Emir Rodríguez Monegal (*23*), and Klaus Müller-Bergh (*21*) have also shown that Carpentier's interest in the avant-garde and association with the surrealist movement in Paris were equally decisive

[4] Jaime Labastida, 'Alejo Carpentier: realidad y conocimiento estético', *Casa de las Américas*, XV, 87 (1974), 21-22.

factors in clarifying his point of view and enabling him to give
his description of America the particular focus encountered in
the novel. As a reflection of the stage to which Carpentier's
thought had progressed, the prologue to *El reino de este mundo*
is an important statement. Yet it poses several problems. Discussion of the chronology of the plot has already revealed certain
discrepancies between the text of the novel and assertions made
in the prologue. In part, however, the problems are also a product of the nature of the prologue itself, which is not a coherent-
ly elaborated theory, but simply a presentation of a series of
preoccupations, expressed in a somewhat rhetorical and un-
systematic way. Although it clearly anticipates his later essay,
'Problemática de la actual novela latinoamericana', the prologue is not a detailed account of the contexts which Carpentier
believed were unique to Latin America. Evidently influenced by
his experiences in France and the lingering need to distance
himself from Surrealism, he identified the uniqueness of Latin
America by referring to a single characteristic, which he called
'lo real maravilloso'.

His attraction to the marvellous was undoubtedly the result of
his contact with Surrealism. In general terms, the concept of the
marvellous implies a sense of wonder produced by unusual,
unexpected, or improbable phenomena. It may occur naturally,
may be the result of deliberate manipulation of reality or its
perception by the artist, or may be produced by magic or supernatural intervention. In any case, it involves the presence of
something different from the normal. This is quite apparent in
the closest that Carpentier comes to a definition:

> ... lo maravilloso comienza a serlo de manera inequívoca
> cuando surge de una inesperada alteración de la realidad
> (el milagro), de una revelación privilegiada de la realidad,
> de una iluminación inhabitual o singularmente
> favorecedora de las inadvertidas riquezas de la realidad, de
> una ampliación de las escalas y categorías de la realidad,
> percibidas con particular intensidad en virtud de una
> exaltación del espíritu que lo conduce a un modo de
> 'estado límite'. (10-11)

Although his definition has a superficial affinity with Surrealism, Carpentier firmly dissociated himself from the Surrealists over the nature and origin of the marvellous and the mechanisms invoked to create it. In a reference to a passage from *Les Chants de Maldoror* by Lautréamont (1846-70), the poet much admired by André Breton and his followers ('el encuentro fortuito del paraguas y de la máquina de coser sobre una mesa de disección', 8), Carpentier condemned the surrealist technique of juxtaposing totally unrelated objects. He criticized the deformation of reality typified by the clocks in Salvador Dali's *The Persistence of Memory* (1931) and by the extravagantly garbed mannequins displayed at the International Surrealist Exhibition in Paris in 1938. He dismissed the Surrealists' admiration of the devices of the fantastic exploited in the Gothic novel and made light of their predilection for inverting reality, as in the painting by Max Ernst, *Two Children Are Theatened by a Nightingale* (1924) (8-9). Carpentier believed that these techniques amounted to a purely artificial sense of the marvellous, 'obtenido con trucos de prestidigitación' (8). By proposing 'lo real maravilloso' as a counter to the surrealist concept of the marvellous, he argued in favour of a natural form that did not entail the arbitrary alteration of reality itself.

Carpentier's reaction against Surrealism was undoubtedly enhanced by the feeling of discovery he experienced when he returned to Cuba from France in 1939 and when he visited Haiti in 1943. Both occasions led him to conclude that the marvellous was the natural patrimony of America: '¿Pero qué es la historia de América toda, sino una crónica de lo real maravilloso?' (17). The combination of the real and the marvellous in episodes of history such as the quest for Eldorado or for the Fountain of Youth were the same qualities that Carpentier discovered in the history of Haiti and endeavoured to reflect in *El reino de este mundo*. Although the events narrated in the novel occurred during the Age of Reason, and belong to the same historical context as the French Revolution, they are beyond the frame of reference of rationalism. Mackandal's rebellion was fomented by class and racial oppression, but was inspired by Voodoo beliefs. In Carpentier's opinion, the effects of the legend of

Mackandal were still to be felt when he visited Haiti in 1943 and had clearly influenced the country's history. Bouckman, Mackandal's successor, led a revolt that ended with independence from France, while the overthrow of Christophe reestablished republicanism in the whole of Haiti. These events and Ti Noel's defiance of the mulatto government are all described in the novel as products of the same beliefs. Thus the founding of a modern nation in the same context as the creation of a myth and the resurgence of primitive beliefs strikes a somewhat dissonant note in an age of revolutionary republicanism. By the same token, the story of a pastrycook who became king, the building of an imitation of the palace of Sans-Souci, and the creation in Haiti of a kingdom modelled on a feudal court of Europe make the history of Henri Christophe appear as an aberration of reality. They constitute, as Carpentier has called them, 'una sucesión de hechos extraordinarios', 'una historia imposible de situar en Europa' (16).

The sense of a distortion of reality inherent in many of the incidents narrated in the novel is a reflection of the combination of several disparate elements in the society described by Carpentier. At the heart of the matter are two unrelated cultural groups: the white Christian Europeans and their black African slaves, followers of Voodoo. Neither group was indigenous to the Caribbean and their differences were further emphasized by socio-economic factors. The dedication of the colonists to the preservation of a hierarchically stratified society as a guarantee of their own freedoms and privileges was at the expense of the slaves and widened the gulf between the two races. The history of Haiti, both during the colonial period and after independence, was also affected by other sources of conflict. While Saint-Domingue was still a French possession it was caught between opposing political philosophies, the ultraconservative pragmatism of the New World colonists and the liberal idealism of the Old World government. After independence, although the French departed, the effects of their regime were still felt. Haiti did not become a racially and culturally homogeneous nation. Its society was affected by the presence of a powerful mulatto population and by the creation of hybrid cultural forms. Moreover, the adoption of European cultural and political practices by the new ruling oligarchy entailed both the preservation of a hierarchically structured society and the perpetuation of social inequality.

The terms 'mestizaje estético', used by Emir Rodríguez Monegal (*23*, pp.646-8), and 'la abolición de las antinomias', used by Gonzalo Celorio (*5*, pp.49-76), very aptly describe the characteristics of Latin America most exploited by Carpentier in writing his novel. He made abundant use of historical situations in which the combination of different and often contradictory circumstances altered the conventional appearance of reality. The two versions of the execution of Mackandal (65-7) are derived from historical sources and are a striking example both of the juxtaposition of two conflicting cultures in Saint-Domingue and of the way in which reality is transformed by one of them. While the colonists who watched Mackandal burn alive were scandalized by the apparent insensitivity of the crowd of negro onlookers, the slaves were in fact rejoicing at having robbed their masters of their prey because they believed that they saw Mackandal take the form of an insect and escape from the fire. The description of Pauline Bonaparte's visit to Saint-Domingue (102-14) is a different example of transformation and contrast. Her initial vision of Saint-Domingue as a tropical paradise is a European idealization of colonial life. When confronted with the real circumstances of life in the colony, however, she undergoes a remarkable change which is reversed only as she sails further from the Caribbean on her return to Europe. Even allowing for the elaboration of his sources, Carpentier's description of Pauline Bonaparte is based on a conflict of different points of view brought together by the conditions of history and is an indication of how perceptions of reality are transformed by environment and distance. Other situations result in more clearly hybrid forms. Carpentier's reference (116) to the priests who began to appear at the close of the war of independence and combined the practices of Catholicism and Voodoo is one example. However, the account of the reign of Henri Christophe, occupying the whole of Part II, is a sustained description of the effects produced by the coalescence of several disparate elements.

In this instance, the impact of the transformation and re-ordering of aspects of reality is appropriately expressed in the astonishment felt by Ti Noel (127), who returned to Haiti after several years in Cuba and discovered a society which contradicted his expectations.

Both the preceding comments and the earlier discussion of the relationship between the novel and its sources confirm that, in addition to the events of history, the context in which they occurred is also reproduced in extended passages of *El reino de este mundo*. In this regard, as Emil Volek correctly observed (*26*, p.160), even the titles of chapters symbolize sources of influence on the history of Haiti. Some refer to Greco-Roman traditions and Christianity ('La hija de Minos y de Pasifae', 'De Profundis'), others to the African background ('La llamada de los caracoles', 'El sacrificio de los toros'), and others ('Dogón dentro del Arca', 'San Trastorno') to the confluence of two cultures. At the same time, several of the titles, to an extent greater than was mentioned by Volek, give an ironic twist to a conventional meaning, as if to exemplify that everything is susceptible to change and distortion. 'Las metamorfosis' do not refer to the mythic tales of Ovid's *Metamorphoses*, but to the myth of Mackandal. 'La hija de Minos y de Pasifae' is not the tragic Phaedra, but the drunken wife of Lenormand. 'Agnus Dei' refers to Ti Noel, not Christ. The irony of some of these titles, 'La hija de Minos y de Pasifae', for example, is also a sign that Carpentier has not limited himself to identifying and simply reproducing the contexts of history. It shows that, in addition to the transformations and effects of 'mestizaje estético' that are a matter of historical record, he obtained equivalent effects from images of his own invention. The first chapter has a particularly illuminating example that is worth commenting on in some detail.

During a visit to Cap Français, Ti Noel has to wait for Lenormand to be shaved. The realistic wax heads, complete with wigs, on a shelf at the entrance to the barber's initially remind Ti Noel of a dummy used by a quack doctor to promote the sale of an elixir for toothache and rheumatism. Then, when he sees some calves' heads arranged on a butcher's counter next door, the wax models prompt him to amuse himself by imagining that 'al lado de las cabezas descoloridas de los terneros, se servían cabezas de blancos señores en el mantel de la misma mesa' (25). Alongside the butcher's is a bookshop with a display of prints outside, among which are several pictures of the head of the King of France and one of an African king receiving a French dignitary. Naturally, Ti Noel compares the qualities of the two monarchs from his own particular point of view. Finally, when Lenormand emerges from the barber's, he buys a calf's head and gives it to Ti Noel to carry. Not only does Lenormand's powdered face now bear a striking resemblance to the barber's wax models, but, according to Ti Noel, the freshly shaved pate under Lenormand's wig must feel remarkably like the calf's head which Ti Noel now has in his hands.

Leaving their thematic implications aside, it is remarkable how this series of images parallels the combination of disparate elements characteristic of the history of Haiti. The heads in Carpentier's description are not intrinsically related, but relationships among them are plausibly created by Ti Noel's observations, Lenormand's visit to the barber and purchase of the calf's head, and by the three shops which, coincidentally but naturally enough, stand side by side. The juxtaposition of a series of disparate objects is therefore achieved without any obvious distortion on the part of the author. The combination of those objects does produce certain transformations, however. Through Ti Noel's rather macabre sense of humour, human heads are placed among those of the calves, and the head of a butchered calf is compared with the head of Lenormand. Finally, Ti Noel's comparison of the prints not only provides the opportunity for juxtaposing the two cultures of Saint-Domingue, but his negative evaluation of the civilized French and correspondingly positive evaluation of the primitive African king are an inversion of conventional perspectives.

Although this example is undoubtedly one of the most complex images of the novel, Carpentier's use of the same methods to imitate the conditions of reality is evident throughout his text. Two further examples, both referring to Lenormand's third wife, Mlle Floridor, will suffice to establish the point. Her portrayal of Phaedra (74-6) reduces Racine's tragedy to the level of the absurd. She is an untalented actress, her performance is given in a drunken stupor, and it is interpreted by her slaves as a confession of her own crimes. Thus an exalted achievement of French culture is converted into a symbol of degradation and is then made to appear all the more decadent in comparison with the negro slaves' creation and preservation of their own culture: 'Ante tantas inmoralidades, los esclavos de la hacienda de Lenormand de Mezy seguían reverenciando a Mackandal. Ti Noel transmitía los relatos del mandinga a sus hijos, enseñándoles canciones muy simples que había compuesto a su gloria, en horas de dar peine y almohaza a los caballos' (76). The brief description of Mlle Floridor when she is found by Lenormand after the slave rebellion is composed of comparable elements: 'Mademoiselle Floridor yacía, despatarrada, sobre la alfombra, con una hoz encajada en el vientre. Su mano muerta agarraba todavía una pata de la cama con gesto cruelmente evocador del que hacía la damisela dormida de un grabado licencioso que, con el título de *El Sueño*, adornaba la alcoba' (88). The juxtaposition of opposites in both examples is within the possible range of combinations that might have occurred in the historical context to which the novel is related. At the same time, the sense of transformation, bordering on parody in both cases, is similar to the kinds of distortion of reality that I have already commented on as characteristic of the history of Haiti.

Carpentier's claim, quoted at the beginning of this chapter, that he was incapable of inventing a story is perhaps more easily understood in the light of his use of these techniques of description. A major part of the narrative is a direct reproduction of history. As I have also shown, the lives of fictional characters are narrated as if they were historical, and hypothetical images of reality are created in agreement with what history will allow. Hence his argument that he does not invent. In this sense, it could fairly be claimed that, for him, fiction is an extension of history and a further means of reproducing it. Curiously enough, however, Carpentier's narration of history relies on the same mechanisms (the juxtaposing of disparate elements, the inversion and distortion of conventional reality) exploited by the

Surrealists whose activities he condemned in the prologue. By the same token, the content of the novel has some of the qualities that the Surrealists admired. Although *El reino de este mundo* is not normally considered a Gothic novel, it reveals an almost Gothic fascination with the macabre and violent. These elements appear in Part I in the severing of Mackandal's arm, the scenes in the house of the Maman Loi, the description of the effects of the poison spread by Mackandal and his followers, the metamorphoses attributed to Mackandal, and his execution by burning at the stake. In Part II, they occur in the midnight conspiracy and Voodoo ceremony, the violent eruption of the slave rebellion, the beheading of Bouckman, the outbreak of yellow fever, and the orgy of violence indulged in by the French before their final surrender of the colony. When looked at solely from the point of view of content, the first two parts of the novel alone reveal a quality of incident, including violence, the exotic, the macabre, and even the supernatural, that would not be misplaced in either Lautréamont's *Les Chants de Maldoror* or Matthew Lewis's *The Monk* (1796). Not only is it tempting to conclude that Carpentier felt a greater attraction to Gothic literature than he admitted, but the techniques of composition and the content of his work reveal a more ambivalent relationship with Surrealism than the vehement condemnation in the prologue would lead us to believe.

Long after the publication of *El reino de este mundo*, Carpentier re-evaluated his association with Surrealism and admitted that the aesthetic sensitivity he acquired from it led him to apply its techniques in developing and portraying his view of Latin America (*20*, pp.21-2). The prologue to the novel is therefore noticeably misleading and lacks the benefit of calm reflection. Carpentier parts company with the Surrealists over the source of the marvellous by claiming that his own work is founded on descriptions that do not entail an artificially improbable distortion of reality. But he misleads the reader of the prologue because he emphasizes this difference and omits any reference to the technical similarity his work still has with Surrealism. At the same time, his own definition of the marvellous is not entirely satisfactory. His criticism of the Surrealists is partly based on the idea that their work is divorced from a belief about the nature of things: 'lo maravilloso invocado en el descreimiento —como lo hicieron los surrealistas durante tantos años— nunca fue sino artimaña literaria' (11-12). In his opinion, 'la sensación de lo maravilloso presupone una fe' (11). It is precisely the notion of faith, to some extent a religious faith, that informs the definition of 'lo real maravilloso' quoted from the prologue earlier in this chapter. Thus, a belief in miracles or in the possibility that a man can change into a wolf is sufficient confirmation for a believer to accept that miracles do happen or that lycanthropy is a real phenomenon. The metamorphoses of Mackandal are therefore proposed as genuine transformations of reality because his followers truly believed in his power to change his form and because their beliefs affected the course of history. When expressed in these terms, however, the sensation of the marvellous is not a universal experience. If it is provoked only when reality is transformed through faith, then its occurrence is limited to relatively few incidents of *El reino de este mundo* and occurs directly only in two chapters of Part I, 'Las metamorfosis' and 'El gran vuelo'. In order to accept the marvellous as a characteristic of the entire novel, it would be necessary to modify this conclusion and propose a different version of 'lo real maravilloso'.

Since the myth of Mackandal sustains the struggle of the negroes throughout the period of history narrated in the novel, there is reason enough to suppose that Carpentier intended the marvellous to be understood as an inherent quality of a greater number of incidents. Indeed, when writing in the final paragraph of the prologue about his fidelity to history he stated that in *El reino de este mundo* 'se narra una sucesión de hechos extraordinarios, ocurridos en la isla de Santo Domingo, en determinada época que no alcanza el lapso de una vida humana, *dejándose que lo maravilloso fluya libremente de una realidad estrictamente seguida en todos sus detalles*' (16). His contention that he had only to be faithful to history in order for the marvellous to appear is supported by a further reference to the quality of the historical elements of the narrative: 'por la dramática singularidad de los acontecimientos, por la fantástica apostura de los personajes que se encontraron, en determinado momento, en la encrucijada mágica de la Ciudad del Cabo, *todo resulta maravilloso*' (16). As my italics show, Carpentier implies that the marvellous is a general characteristic and not a matter of faith alone. On this basis, we must broaden our conception of 'lo real maravilloso' to include the effects produced by the juxtaposing of disparate elements, the distortions of conventional reality, and the inversions of normal perceptions referred to in this chapter, which are to be traced to the historical conditions of Haiti. In fact, it is only through such a broad definition that any appropriate meaning can be given to the rhetorical question at the end of the prologue and to Carpentier's suggestion that the entire history of America is 'una crónica de lo real maravilloso' (17).

On the basis of these considerations, the prologue appears to propose two conceptually contradictory versions of 'lo real maravilloso'. If it is the product of the verifiable phenomena of history, it is phenomenological, but, if it is derived from the persistence in Latin America of a belief in the validity of myth, its sources are ontological (that is, they are concerned with the philosophical basis of reality). As if this contradiction were not enough, it is also necessary to ask whether or not either version does in fact provoke a sense of the marvellous. For the marvellous to exist, it must be experienced by someone, and, if it is a product of faith, this experience is the privilege of believers. As the two versions of the execution show quite clearly, the metamorphoses of Mackandal in *El reino de este mundo* are known only to the negro slaves, in whose religion lycanthropy is an accepted phenomenon. Since lycanthropy is accepted by the negroes, however, its manifestation is not a marvellous transformation of reality but a confirmation of what they believe is the natural order of things. To the negroes of Haiti, therefore, Mackandal's powers are neither surprising nor marvellous. Nor are they to the reader of the novel, although for different reasons. The reader is persuaded to attribute them to a religious belief and, particularly in the case of the two versions of Mackandal's execution, is provided with a rational explanation: he did not really escape but only broke loose momentarily from the bonds that held him to the stake (65-6). Mackandal's metamorphoses and escape would perhaps have produced a sensation of the marvellous and a genuine transformation of reality if they had also been experienced by the European colonists or if the reader had been left with an element of uncertainty, not knowing whether or not they actually occurred. Such a possibility, however, would necessarily require us to change Carpentier's definition quite radically and to suggest that the marvellous does not presuppose a certain faith but the lack of it.

Even when the marvellous is considered from a phenomenological point of view, as a product of historical circumstances in Haiti, it is still a beleaguered concept. The history of Haiti only appears to be marvellous in the light of a comparison with Europe in which the latter has the status of a conventional standard. It is the deviation from this standard that evokes a sensation of the marvellous, a point implicitly acknowledged by Carpentier when he stated in the prologue that the novel is 'una historia imposible de situar en Europa' (16). America, then, is not inherently marvellous, but simply appears to be so to a non-American who judges from the perspective of his belief about how reality should be constituted. Many of the transformations of reality produced by the circumstances of history in Haiti already referred to in this chapter are the result of an implied comparison between Europe and America and are sufficient to indicate the extent to which the content of the novel as a whole is affected. I have also alluded to the outsider's perception of matters from a different angle. It is exemplified in the novel by Lenormand (73) and Pauline Bonaparte, whose attitudes change according to whether they see things from the perspective of Europe or of the colony. Above all, it is illustrated by Ti Noel's return to Haiti from Cuba after a prolonged absence. His astonishment at Christophe's regime is that of the outsider whose expectations are challenged by appearances that cannot be immediately accommodated within an existing frame of reference. To some extent, Ti Noel's condition is comparable to that of Carpentier himself. After a prolonged absence from America, he, too, returned as an outsider. Not surprisingly, he fell into the trap that has caught many writers in Latin America

since the time of the conquest. Like them, perhaps even as a consequence of immersing himself in the literature of the conquest
and colonial period while in Paris, he saw America through
European eyes. The marvellousness he sought to describe is
therefore not autonomous to Latin America but is the product
of an external frame of reference. His claim that the entire
history of America is 'una crónica de lo real maravilloso' (17)
does not take this fact into account and does not acknowledge
that the history of America often appears to be marvellous
because it was frequently written by Europeans who had difficulty in accommodating the New World to their own
preconception of reality.

'Lo real maravilloso' is also an unsatisfactory term because it
was coined with two purposes in mind. In addition to defining
the character of Latin America, it was intended to counter the
excesses of Surrealism with a form of the marvellous dependent
on the natural manifestations of reality. Given the difficulties it
creates when applied to the novel, however, it is not surprising to
find that the term has less importance in Carpentier's later
writing. Nevertheless, the continuity of his thought from the
prologue of *El reino de este mundo* to 'Problemática de la actual
novela latinoamericana' is quite evident. Much of the later essay
is based on a comparison between Europe and America, but
Carpentier's description of the contexts and baroque qualities of
the New World entail a significant clarification of the position
previously adopted in the prologue. His commentary on the *contextos* of Latin America is a much clearer discussion of his ideas
about how the conditions of reality should be accurately portrayed by the writer. At the same time, his reference to the baroque is a further acknowledgement of his belief that Latin
America is characterized by the convergence of innumerable
disparate elements from a variety of cultural sources. Above all,
the need to justify his stance as an aesthetic alternative to
Surrealism is no longer necessary. As a result, although the real
is still the focus of Carpentier's attention, it is no longer related
to the marvellous.

Whatever the problems associated with 'lo real maravilloso',
they should not be compounded by overlooking differences bet-

ween Carpentier's description of reality and that of other novelists. There is a tendency among critics to treat different forms of departure from conventional realism in the contemporary Spanish American novel as responses to the same concepts. In Gonzalo Celorio's comparative study (5) of Surrealism and 'lo real maravilloso', for example, the latter term is applied to the work of Gabriel García Márquez, Miguel Angel Asturias, Juan Rulfo, and Carpentier. Roberto González Echevarría, on the other hand, rightly saw the need to differentiate between the concepts on which Carpentier based his formulation of 'lo real maravilloso' and other approaches to the description of reality. His commentary on the history of the term magical realism (8, pp.109-29) is particularly instructive, but still leaves some problems. He argues that there are two versions of magical realism. The first, phenomenological in nature, is a product of perception and was derived from a book on Post-Expressionist painting by the German art critic Franz Roh.[5] The second is Carpentier's 'lo real maravilloso', which was formed against the background of Surrealism, is based on faith and is ontological in nature. Since I have shown that Carpentier's work, as González Echevarría admits in passing (8, p.115), has the properties of both versions, it seems appropriate to call *El reino de este mundo* a magical realist novel which presumably has something in common with other novels defined by the same term. Yet there are reasons for questioning this supposition. Regardless of any affinity with the work of Franz Roh, Carpentier did not use his terminology. Moreover, the term magical realism has been appropriated by critics of the contemporary novel in circumstances that are clearly dissociated from the context in which it was employed by Franz Roh. It is a discredited term which has been used somewhat indiscriminately to designate almost any departure from conventional realism characterized by descriptions of unusual phenomena or by mythology, fantasy, magic, or the supernatural. To reconstitute the definition of magical realism

[5] *Nach-Expressionismus (Magischer Realismus): Probleme der neuesten Europäischen Malerei* (Leipzig, 1925). Roh's book was certainly known to Carpentier through the Spanish translation published in Madrid by Revista de Occidente in 1927 *(Realismo mágico: postexpresionismo. Problemas de la pintura europea más reciente)*.

and rehabilitate it as a useful critical term is an arduous task that has yet to be undertaken satisfactorily. For the purpose of discussing *El reino de este mundo*, therefore, an important premise must be adopted: the magical realism of Franz Roh is subsumed by 'lo real maravilloso' of Alejo Carpentier and is not the same magical realism of more recent criticism. In order to verify in what sense the latter may be applicable to Carpentier, a brief comparison between *El reino de este mundo* and another novel conventionally termed magical realist will be sufficient. *Cien años de soledad* (1967), by the Colombian novelist Gabriel García Márquez, will serve this purpose.

Since Carpentier endeavoured to remain as faithful as possible to his sources, both the conduct of characters and the description of incidents in *El reino de este mundo* are constrained by conditions imposed by recorded history. Carpentier did not seek to transform history, but to narrate it and to describe its attributes. Nor did he try to create myths, but to identify those already in existence. The author of *Cien años de soledad* exploited history quite differently, however. Although it is still possible to collate the novel with the history of Colombia, García Márquez was not bound by his sources. He overstepped the limits of empirical reality and existing mythology and invented his own versions. Thus, the image of reality portrayed in *Cien años de soledad* acquires a meaning that depends on the internal structure of the world created by García Márquez. By contrast, the image of reality portrayed in *El reino de este mundo*, in principle at least, is derived from Carpentier's opinion of a world external to the novel. This difference must obviously be taken into account in any comparison of the two works, and is particularly important if the purpose of comparison is to define the role of the marvellous and to establish a relationship with the avant-garde movements of the twenties and thirties.

Although the marvellous is relevant to both novelists, they approached it from different angles and obtained different results. García Márquez broadened the scope of reality by making the marvellous part of it. As an integral part of his narrative, he introduced many inexplicable phenomena that are contrary to nature but are described as if they were everyday occurrences.

For this reason alone, if magical is defined as a term referring to phenomena that occur in violation of natural laws, *Cien años de soledad* deserves to be called a magical realist novel. *El reino de este mundo* is not generally characterized by the same quality. When considered as a product of faith, the notion of 'lo real maravilloso' entails the description of unreal phenomena that may be perceived as real by a certain group of people. Its purpose is to identify the presence of the marvellous in reality without changing reality itself or broadening its scope. Incidents such as those pertaining to a belief in the myth of Mackandal are therefore to be accepted as literal transcriptions of the real world. In *Cien años de soledad*, however, the re-appearance of characters after their death, the ascension of Remedios la Bella, or the miraculous levitation of a priest are accepted as mundane events and must either be interpreted symbolically or metaphorically or be seen as parts of a story, to some extent comparable to a fairy-story or a mythical tale, in which the normal laws of nature are no longer operable.

The suspension of natural laws in *El reino de este mundo* occurs only in its final episodes. The metamorphoses of Ti Noel in the last two chapters do not have the same connotations as those of Mackandal in Part I. Although a belief in the lycanthropic powers of Mackandal is reported in the histories of Haiti, his actual experiences while transformed into an animal are neither recorded in history, nor described in the novel. Ever faithful to his sources, Carpentier only recorded the negroes' belief that the metamorphoses did occur and thereby preserved the integrity of empirical reality. In the case of Ti Noel, however, Carpentier exploited the fact that he is a fictional character whose portrayal is not so dependent on historical sources. The metamorphoses of Ti Noel are founded on the precedent set by a belief in Mackandal's ability (190) and, as such, perpetuate in fiction the myth that originated in historical circumstances. But, in this instance, rather than merely recording a belief in lycanthropy, Carpentier described Ti Noel's experiences. As a result, there is a significant change in the quality of the narrative: the marvellous reality of history that characterizes the belief in the myth of Mackandal becomes the magical reality of fiction when the myth is realized through the experiences of Ti Noel. Such an evolution also yields a corresponding adjustment in interpretation. Although the narrative preceding the last two chapters can generally be read, with appropriate reservations to allow for the fictional elements, as a literal transcription of history, the last two chapters cannot be read in exactly the same way. They have a clear metaphorical meaning, which is explained in the text (196-7) and which gives Ti Noel and the reader a basis for interpreting both the myth of Mackandal and the history of Haiti.

The preceding comments do not solve all the problems associated with 'lo real maravilloso' and magical realism. The two terms should be examined and defined in a broader context before either of them can be satisfactorily used to categorize contemporary works of fiction in Spanish America. Yet, it is possible to reach some conclusions with regard to *El reino de este mundo*. Both 'lo real maravilloso' and 'magical realism' are applicable to the novel, although neither is sufficient by itself to characterize the quality of realism in the novel as a whole. Our observations on the metamorphoses of Mackandal and Ti Noel, however, are a suitable basis for differentiating between the two terms. Regardless of its problems, 'lo real maravilloso' is applicable to the greater part of the narrative and indicates a description of reality based on empiricism, in which myth is identified as a belief capable of influencing the course of history. Magical realism is applicable only to the final episodes of the novel. Free of the restrictions of empiricism, it entails the re-enactment of myth and the creation of a metaphor through which an interpretation of history is conveyed. The fact that *El reino de este mundo* cannot be exclusively categorized as an example of just one of these two possibilities is not necessarily an unsatisfactory conclusion. The presence in the novel, in the proportions I have stated, of both 'lo real maravilloso' and magical realism is an indication of Carpentier's intention of describing reality in order to discover the meaning underlying its appearances. In this sense, he may by appropriately categorized as a precursor of later novelists, such as García Márquez, whose work consists in a more elaborate attempt to describe reality exclusively in terms of its hidden meaning.[6]

---

[6] Several essays on 'lo real maravilloso' have come to my attention since completing this Critical Guide. Two by Irlemar Chiampi are particularly worth consulting: 'Alejo Carpentier y el surrealismo', *Revista de la Universidad de México*, XXXVII, 5 (1981), 2-10, and *O realismo maravilhoso: forma e ideologia no romance hispano-americano* (São Paulo: Editora Perspectiva, 1980). The first sheds light on contacts between Carpentier and Surrealism that had hitherto passed unnoticed; the second, in Portuguese, is a systematic study intended to establish a theory of 'lo real maravilloso'. Frederick de Armas, in 'Metamorphosis as Revolt: Cervantes' *Persiles y Sigismunda* and Carpentier's *El reino de este mundo*', *Hispanic Review*, XLIX (1981), 297-316, presents an interesting comparison of the role of the marvellous in the two authors and also touches on its relation to narrative technique, a subject dealt with more fully by Steven Bell in 'Carpentier's *Reino de este mundo* in a New Light: Toward a Theory of the Fantastic', *Journal of Spanish Studies: Twentieth Century*, VIII (1980), 29-43.

4. Structure and Meaning

In the preceding chapters I have established the extent to which Carpentier remained faithful to his sources when writing *El reino de este mundo*. We have also seen that the novel is related to the author's perception of the aesthetic connotations of American history and his opinion of its appropriateness as a fit subject for literature. But, just as the novel is not an exact reproduction of history, it is also more than an attempt to exemplify a personal thesis about the nature of creative writing. While the comment that *El reino de este mundo* is a work of literature is, of course, somewhat banal, it properly draws attention to its fundamental character. As a work of literature, the novel has a degree of autonomy and should not be interpreted exclusively in the light of either the circumstances of its composition or the relation of content to sources. Although an investigation of the origin of Carpentier's work and an evaluation of his aesthetic principles help to verify how the novel was written and assist in the task of intepretation, they do not automatically reveal all that we wish to know about its meaning and structure. On the grounds that history is not adhered to fully or is viewed from a very particular angle, it could be argued that, in spite of the comments in the prologue, Carpentier distorts reality. On the other hand, if *El reino de este mundo* is considered principally as a literary text, the view of reality it conveys must be assessed according to criteria that both allow for the methods of description permitted to literature and attribute a proper significance to the distortion that these entail.

A literary text is not an exact reproduction of reality, but a metaphor presented through language, a poetic transformation of the real. As such, it explores the meaning of things by describing a cosmos structured according to rules that differ from those prevailing in the real world. By establishing its own rules, the text diminishes the absolute importance of sources, which undergo a poetic transformation and acquire a new sense of coherence directly related to their organization in the text. Carpentier's use of history and description of America in accordance with the concept of 'lo real maravilloso' are evidence that the sources of *El reino de este mundo* are transformed. While his statements in the prologue confirm the connection between the text and a certain historical reality, they omit all reference to the nature of this connection. They do not acknowledge that the relationship between them is essentially metonymic (that is, it substitutes one thing for another to which it is closely related) because it is based on a conscious selection and organization of the elements of reality that best convey the author's view. An examination of the structure of *El reino de este mundo*, therefore, will not only help to describe some of the characteristics of the text, its unity and the relations between its different parts, but will also show how the novel conveys a message which sheds light on a particular segment of reality.

Apart from a conception of the literary text as a metaphor of reality, the need to establish principles explaining the underlying coherence given to history in *El reino de este mundo* is also derived from earlier comparison of the novel with its sources. In the light of that comparison, exclusive reliance on history as the basis of the organization of the text poses several difficulties. Not only is the passage of historical time distorted by the absence of dates and the telescoping of time, but significant periods in the history of Haiti, although part of the total period covered by the novel, are either omitted entirely or referred to only in passing. Such is the case of the rise to power of Toussaint Louverture, the immediate outcome of the war of independence, the rule of Jean-Jacques Dessalines, the early part of the reign of Henri Christophe, and the reunification of Haiti under the presidency of Jean-Pierre Boyer. Finally, Carpentier's selective use of sources is complicated by countless esoteric references to minor historical details and his tendency to blur the distinction between fact and fiction. The combination of all these factors raises doubts concerning the possible role of history in the reception and interpretation of the text by the reader. A reading of the novel is undoubtedly enriched by a knowledge of the period in which it is set, but is not dependent on it. Although Carpentier appeals more to an informed reader, his message is nonetheless accessible to one who reads his work without the benefit of a detailed knowledge of its historical background. In a further analysis of *El reino de este mundo*, I shall examine the limitations of a reading of the text dependent on its sources and shall suggest an interpretation which, without discounting the relevance of sources, shows Carpentier's concern for a much broader context than the history of a single country.

Cyclical Structures

Since Carpentier stresses the reiterative quality of events, *El reino de este mundo* is not, strictly speaking, a linear history of Haiti from the mid-eighteenth century to just beyond the first quarter of the nineteenth. He has selected events from this period on the basis of the repetition they entail and has emphasized this quality when describing them in the novel. The criteria he employed in selecting events and organizing them in the text are consequently of considerable interest. Among those who have approached the matter from the perspective of history and chronology, Roberto González Echevarría offers one of the most complex analyses (*8*, pp.129-47). He argues that the novel has a cyclical structure initially determined by history and the occurrence on comparable dates of events that have a common significance but are widely separated in time. He also proposes that Carpentier reinforced this structure by modifying several dates and by locating the narration of events in the novel so that incidents of parallel significance occupy parallel positions in the text when its twenty-six chapters are considered as a single sequence divided into two consecutive cycles of thirteen chapters each. In the light of his analysis, he suggests that this structure has important implications concerning Carpentier's concept of the marvellous:

> Magic, the marvelous, would be the relation between the numerical disposition of historical events and the text, a relation between those two orders whose transparent mediator would be Carpentier. By this relation the separa-

tion between being and cosmos mentioned by [Octavio] Paz when speaking of Surrealism could be transcended and the relation itself could constitute the credible, documentable miracle sustaining the faith that Carpentier speaks about in the prologue. The presence of such a relation could also allow one to speak of the marvelous as being inscribed in the text without the benefit of a systematic effort on the part of a reflexive consciousness to do so. (*8*, pp.145-6)

At the same time, acknowledging Carpentier's own intervention in history, González Echevarría offers a more radical conclusion: 'The text is the creation of an ornate order with pretensions of permanence, but constituted with the bad faith of its ultimate and imminent dissolution, as when its system is pressed to the limit of meaning and dissolves into chaos and formlessness' (*8*, p.147).

Some of the problems raised by González Echevarría's analysis will be referred to in the course of the following comments, but his conclusion concerning the marvellous must be dealt with more immediately. The reflexive consciousness of Carpentier looms over the whole of *El reino de este mundo*. It is he who selected the historical incidents included in the novel and omitted others, who accepted them as they were or altered them, and who created whatever parallels arise from the disposition of chapters. In these terms alone, it is difficult to acccept that the marvellous is 'inscribed in the text without the benefit of a systematic effort on the part of a reflexive consciousness to do so'. Moreover, the marvellous cannot be 'the relation between the numerical disposition of historical events and the text' because the possibility of such a relation has been disposed of by Carpentier. Among the major characteristics of the novel are its uncertain chronology and the absence of dates. As a result, the 'numerical' disposition of history is dismantled. By reconstituting it as the basis of the novel, González Echevarría introduces the very element with which the text dispenses.

He proposes, for instance, that Bouckman's rebellion and the fall of Christophe are related by the symmetry of their dates.

Bouckman's conspiracy occurred on Sunday, 14 August 1791, and the rebellion erupted on Monday, 22 August, eight days later. However, these dates can be found only in the historical sources; the novel alludes only to August as the month in which the conspiracy was held (77) and to the lapse of eight days before the outbreak of the rebellion (80). González Echevarría's reading of the chapters concerning the death of Henri Christophe allowed him to propose that the King suffered a stroke on Sunday, 15 August 1820, and committed suicide a week later on Sunday, 22 August. However, neither history nor the novel supports that reading entirely. According to tradition, Christophe suffered a stroke while attending mass on Assumption Day. The text appropriately refers to 15 August, but does not give the year and does not state that it was a Sunday. Moreover, the day of the week cannot be deduced from the text solely through reference to the Assumption. Unlike the Ascension of Christ, with which González Echevarría inadvertently confused it (*8*, p.138) and which, in any case, is traditionally commemorated forty days after Easter on a Thursday, the Assumption is not a movable feast. In fact, although some sources do place it on a Sunday, August 15 fell on a Tuesday in 1820. History confirms that Christophe died on a Sunday, but on 8 October 1820, not 22 August which, of course, was also a Tuesday. Although the text refers to a Sunday (153), it does not permit the decisive conclusion that Carpentier actually adjusted the date to establish a parallel with the slave rebellion. The reference in question, 'el domingo siguiente', at the beginning of the chapter in which Christophe's death is described, possibly alludes to the time elapsed since the events of the preceding chapter, dated 15 August, but does not, of course, permit the conclusion that 15 August was also a Sunday. Given the absence of a clear chronology throughout *El reino de este mundo*, 'el domingo siguiente' could equally refer to a Sunday following an unspecified occasion. In this case, it could implicitly allude to Sunday, 8 October 1820, the date of Christophe's death that Carpentier would have found in his sources. The internal chronology of the novel, however, establishes only one certain parallel between Bouckman and Christophe, namely that the conspiracy led by the former and the stroke suffered by the latter occurred in August of different years. To take matters further requires us to interpret the text in the light of information it does not contain and does not necessarily suggest. As will be shown, the parallels among incidents narrated in the novel are based not on when they occurred but on what they imply.

Although certain aspects of the symmetrical pattern proposed by González Echevarría are still intriguing, his overall design loses some of its appeal when history and the text are properly confronted. The importance he attaches to Sundays, for example, is also weakened by omission from the text of any allusion to the fact that the Christmas Day on which Mackandal reappeared and was captured was indeed a Sunday. Without this information, the only relevance we can attribute to the date is that which is symbolically implied by the return of a potential voodoo saviour on the same day that the birth of Christ is commemorated. The actual day of the week and the year, however, are not important and are not mentioned. In addition to these problems, the symmetrical design based on the numerical order of the chapters is less conclusive than González Echevarría's analysis shows. The main problem is the role of the thirteenth chapter as the centre of the novel. Since there are twenty-six chapters in total, the thirteenth cannot be exactly the 'mathematical' (*8*, 142) centre. Its status as the chronological centre is also questionable. The thirteenth chapter describes the life of Lenormand and Ti Noel in Santiago de Cuba. Since the sources confirm that they could have reached Santiago during the latter half of 1791, their arrival is the centre of a period from 1753 to 1828, the outside dates suggested by González Echevarría for the entire novel. It is also the centre of the period 1751-1830, the approximate dates of the period I have proposed for the duration of events for the entire novel. However, the events of 1791 are also described in three other chapters, the tenth, eleventh, and twelfth, which are concerned with the slave rebellion. Typically, the year is not mentioned in the text. Moreover, as noted in the discussion of the chronology of the novel, the duration of the thirteenth chapter is quite uncertain. Although its beginning, the arrival in Santiago, can be placed in

1791, it is impossible to be so precise about the rest of the chapter, which could conceivably extend to 1803. Certainly the dogs seen by Ti Noel at the beginning of the fourteenth chapter were sent to Saint-Domingue in that year. The main problem, then, is that *El reino de este mundo* reproduces history without reproducing its chronology in a form that is accessible to the reader. As a result, although 1791 is acceptable as the possible centre of the period covered by the novel, the chronological centre of the novel itself is much more elusive. The role of the thirteenth and fourteenth chapters at the centre is thematic rather than chronological. While the thirteenth chapter concludes the first half of the text with an account of the life of the exiles in Cuba, the fourteenth begins the second half by returning the reader's attention to Saint-Domingue and initiating a second cycle of events. Strictly speaking, the centre of the novel, both formally and mathematically, is the interval between the two chapters, between the end of one sequence of events and the beginning of another. González Echevarría's demonstration that events in the novel conform to two comparable cycles is therefore helpful, although his complex numerical calculations are excessive. Similarly, the text is based on 'the creation of an ornate order' which tends to disintegrate when confronted with history. But disintegration occurs because history is narrated from a very particular point of view. Carpentier took the chronology of history into account when writing the novel, but his submersion of it in the text is an important element in a poetic transformation of reality and the creation of a new order as a more suitable vehicle for the meaning he wished to convey. As Emile Volek suggested (*26*, p.150), this order and its meaning are to be sought initially in the artistic structure of the text.

The reader of *El reino de este mundo* cannot fail to notice the formal disposition of the text. It has four parts, with eight, seven, seven, and four chapters respectively. At first glance, the numbers are arbitrary, but there is an underlying equilibrium. The images and associations evoked in the first chapter by Ti Noel's visit to Cap Français are emblematic of the novel as a whole and introduce the major themes of the text. The incidents which constitute the plot begin with the mutilation of

Mackandal in the second chapter. By omitting the first chapter from our calculations, the events of the first three parts of the novel are therefore narrated in three sequences of seven chapters each. The fact that the final part has only four chapters reflects its role at the end of the novel. Just as the first chapter is an introduction, the final ones are a conclusion. They tie a number of loose ends remaining in the plot, convey a synthesis of the meaning of the work, and anticipate the continuation of events beyond the end of the novel. This equilibrium in the disposition of the text means that none of the four parts is emphasized more than any other. All are relatively autonomous and constitute a series of new beginnings in the narrative. Each is separated from the others by an epigraph and a lapse in time that is evident in the text even if its duration must be verified in the sources. In addition to a particular sequence of events, the narrative is also composed of four extended images, juxtaposed by their inclusion in the same text. Not surprisingly, it reflects the methods of description associated with Carpentier's concept of 'lo real maravilloso'.

The division of the novel into four parts corresponds to the way in which its content is developed. The heads contemplated by Ti Noel in the first chapter, a reminder, perhaps, of the prophetic qualities attributed to art by the Surrealists, are a premonition of things to come. The severed heads evoke both the most recognizable symbol of the French Revolution and the general context of a significant part of the novel. The violence of social change is thereby poetically conveyed at the outset. Ti Noel's comparison of the pictures of the French and African monarchs, his denigration of the former and exaltation of the latter, implies an aspiration for an ideal. Although never realized, its pursuit in the four major historical episodes of the novel, one in each part, fulfills the prophecy of revolution evoked by the heads. The revolt led by Mackandal, described in Part I, is unsuccessful. It converts Mackandal into a legendary figure who will inspire future rebellions, but leaves the existing social order intact. Another revolt is needed. In Part II, the rebellion initiated by Bouckman succeeds in driving out the French and liberating the slaves, but does not culminate in an ideal social

order. Since life under Henri Christophe, as described in Part
III, amounts to the re-establishment of an earlier social structure, it, too, must be challenged and overthrown. The Mulatto
Republic that follows is equally unsatisfactory. Although a
rebellion against it is only announced in Part IV, it is clear that
the need for a continued revolutionary movement is still alive.
Indeed, the conclusion reached by Ti Noel before his death is
that man's life in the kingdom of this world is a continuous
struggle in search of a better order.

The four parts of the novel are a single theme and its varia-
tions: revolution is followed by the return of the conditions that
were initially challenged and a new revolt is required. The
general movement of the plot is therefore cyclical, a quality
enhanced by the division of the text into four parts and by the
uses of history already mentioned. By selecting only certain
episodes of history, by omitting their dates and the length of
time that separates them, and by constituting the four parts as
relatively autonomous units, Carpentier invites the reader to sus-
pend his view of events as a chronological continuum. The new
order given to history, the same order that sustains the text,
stresses the reiterative quality of events and de-emphasizes their
character as a sequential series. This conclusion generally coin-
cides with that reached by Emil Volek, even if he reached it by
different means. He identifies two major divisions in the text. Its
conclusion, or interpretation, is contained in the final one and a
half chapters. The entire earlier part of the novel, consisting of
the argument, or illustration of the problem, is based on three
cycles, represented by the white colonists, King Christophe, and
the Mulatto Republic. Volek's comments on their relation bear
repeating:

> ...se comienza con la ilusión de la libertad y sigue su propio
> ciclo, es decir, el ascenso y la caída (siendo completo el de
> los colonos y parciales los demás: en el de Henri
> Christophe observamos la fase descendente, en el de los
> mulatos la ascendente).
>
> El ciclo completo de los colonos es de carácter introduc-
> torio y ejemplar, representa la clave del 'argumento'. En

cuanto a los demás, el autor escoge sólo lo sustancial que
baste para producir la ilusión del todo y expresar la idea
básica del 'argumento', o sea, el movimiento cíclico. (*26*,
pp.157-8)

Volek's pattern differs from the one I have proposed, but does
not contradict it. A further examination of the content of *El
reino de este mundo* reveals a complex network of parallels
which consolidate the notion of cyclical movement and
demonstrate that the cyclical structure of the novel occurs on
several levels. In addition to the four cycles of revolution, the
novel contains a single complete cycle, two parallel cycles, and a
series of more random repetitions.

The central motif of the single cycle is the life of Ti Noel. He is
the only character whose existence spans all events, and each of
the four parts portrays him at a different stage in his life. As
Emma Speratti-Piñero has demonstrated (*24*), his life is akin to
an apprenticeship begun under the guidance of Mackandal in the
first chapters of the novel and continued through the experiences
of a lifetime. The last chapter describes the culmination of the
process and reveals that Ti Noel finally understands what he
began to learn under the tutelage of Mackandal. His metamorphoses, a clear echo of those of his master, connect the end of
the novel to its beginning and give the impression of a completed
cycle. At the same time, Ti Noel's realization that metamorphosis is a means not of evading responsibility but of continuing
the struggle for liberation, provides a basis for interpreting the
cycle of events that occurs during his lifetime. He learns that
there is no fundamental distinction between the world of nature
and the world of men. The different versions of the natural
kingdom witnessed during his metamorphoses and the different
forms of human society observed in the course of his life are all
rigid hierarchies, of which he is always a victim. Although set in
the Caribbean, the cycle traced by his life is certainly intended to
reflect a more universal condition. Most immediately, it is comparable to the history of Latin American countries which have
undergone a similar cycle of changes and have experienced a colonial regime, a struggle for independence, a period of *caudi-*

llismo, and the emergence of a mixed or *mestizo* society. But the meaning of Ti Noel's life is not necessarily limited to Latin America. In a moment of lucidity at the end of his life, when he becomes aware of the implications of his experiences, he feels as if he has carried the burden of all humanity:

> Vivió, en el espacio de un pálpito, los momentos capitales de su vida; volvió a ver a los héroes que le habían revelado la fuerza y la abundancia de sus lejanos antepasados del Africa, haciéndole creer en las posibles germinaciones del porvenir. Se sintió viejo de siglos incontables. Un cansancio cósmico, de planeta cargado de piedras, caía sobre sus hombros descarnados por tantos golpes, sudores y rebeldías. (196)

In the light of Ti Noel's conclusions and the implication that his experiences are those of universal man, it is appropriate to give an interim assessment of the novel. Since Ti Noel's life encompasses a series of cyclical repetitions, it seems correct to conclude that all progress is relative and that significant changes are an illusion. This conclusion is also supported by Carpentier's use of the myth of Sisyphus in his fiction as an image of the burden of existence. Although not referred to directly in *El reino de este mundo*, the myth is implied both by the description of the forced labourers carrying the bricks up the mountain for the construction of Christophe's citadel (134-5) and at the end of the novel, when human existence is referred to as endless toil and sacrifice. However, the novel does not convey such an entirely pessimistic view. *El reino de este mundo* has a closed narrative in the sense that no matters of plot are left unresolved at the end. The lives of all the characters are completed, and the cyclone, the green wind that blows from the ocean (198), eliminates even the last vestiges of Ti Noel. But the march of history remains open. When Ti Noel reviews the small accomplishments of his own life, he understands that, although he has seen little progress, he has witnessed the indomitability of the human spirit and the struggle for a brighter future. He not only implies that the struggle will continue, but his last act is a call for rebellion against the tyranny of the mulatto regime. Moreover, the final lines of the novel have an element of ambiguity. As some critics have suggested (*24*, p.227; *26*, pp.166-7), the vulture that flies into the Bois Caimán at the very end of the novel is perhaps a further incarnation of Ti Noel, much like the final metamorphosis of Mackandal, that will ensure the survival of a spirit of rebellion. Thus, although we may conclude that Carpentier's view of history is of a series of repetitive cycles, we may also agree with critics who have suggested that, rather than the enclosed form of the circle, the cycles follow the trajectory of a spiral, so that history is not entirely static but remains open to the future. This possibility and the more universal implications of the meaning of the novel will be further discussed later in this chapter.

The event that divides *El reino de este mundo* into two parallel cycles is the loss of the colony by the French settlers to the negro slaves and the mulattoes. While the first half of the novel (Parts I and II) is an account of white colonial rule, the second (Parts III and IV) describes life after independence under black and mulatto government. On this basis, the differences between the two halves are matters of race and political power. But the text invites the reader to overlook such differences and to notice certain fundamental similarities. This is achieved initially by omitting an account of the years between the end of the colonial period and the later years of Christophe's reign so that the two follow each other as if placed side by side for comparison. Numerous parallels between the two halves of the text consolidate their similarity and convey the impression that the second half of the novel repeats much of what has already appeared in the first.

Parts I and III contain the beginnings of the two sequences. At the beginning of each part Ti Noel contemplates the characteristics of monarchy. The unexpected sight that confronts him when he discovers the palace at Millot (125-9) shortly after his return from Cuba calls to mind the images of the French court and its artificiality, conveyed by the prints outside the bookseller's described at the beginning of the novel (25-9):

Pero lo que más asombraba a Ti Noel era el descubrimien-

to de que ese mundo prodigioso, como no lo habían conocido los gobernadores franceses del Cabo, era un mundo
de negros. Porque negras eran aquellas hermosas señoras,
de firme nalgatorio, que ahora bailaban la rueda en torno
a una fuente de tritones; negros aquellos dos ministros de
medias blancas, que descendían, con la cartera de becerro
debajo del brazo, la escalinata de honor; negro aquel
cocinero, con cola de armiño en el bonete, que recibía un
venado de hombros de varios aldeanos conducidos por el
Montero Mayor; negros aquellos húsares que trotaban en
el picadero;... (127)

The one significant difference, as the preceding passage shows,
is that Christophe's courtiers are black. But this is precisely the
difference that emphasizes the cyclical return of events.
Although Christophe's courtiers are of African origin, his
kingdom is not and bears no likeness to the African monarchy
imagined by Ti Noel from Mackandal's stories and the prints he
looked at outside the shop in Cap Français so many years
before. In spite of the belief that life in Haiti has improved, Ti
Noel soon discovers that the opposite is true. The only real
change is his enslavement by new masters of the same race as he.
The full impact of his discovery is felt when he is made to carry
bricks as part of the labour gang working on the construction of
the citadel at La Ferrière. When he compares his plight to his
earlier status as a slave, he realizes that he has gained nothing
and that the society to which he has returned, although differently disguised, is fundamentally the same as the one he knew
before:

Andando, andando, de arriba abajo y de abajo arriba, el
negro comenzó a pensar que las orquestas de cámara de
Sans-Souci, el fausto de los uniformes y las estatuas de
blancas desnudas que se calentaban al sol sobre sus zócalos
de almocárabes, entre los bojes tallados de los canteros, se
debían a una esclavitud tan abominable como la que había
conocido en la hacienda de Monsieur Lenormand de Mezy.
(134)

The antipathy consequently felt by Ti Noel toward Henri Christophe is a recurrence of an earlier sentiment referred to first at the beginning of the novel in a passage describing Ti Noel and Lenormand on their way home from Cap Français:

> Ti Noel ... tarareó para sus adentros una copla marinera, muy cantada por los toneleros del puerto, en que se echaban mierdas al rey de Inglaterra. De lo último sí estaba seguro, aunque la letra no estuviese en *créole*. Por lo mismo, la sabía. Además, tan poca cosa era para él el rey de Inglaterra como el de Francia o el de España, que mandaba en la otra mitad de la isla, y cuyas mujeres —según afirmaba Mackandal— se enrojecían las mejillas con sangre de buey y enterraban fetos de infantes en un convento cuyos sótanos estaban llenos de esqueletos rechazados por el cielo verdadero, donde no se querían muertos ignorantes de los dioses verdaderos. (30-1)

The essential elements of this passage are recalled in Part III and are also placed in the context of a journey home to Cap Français. During the later visit Ti Noel witnesses the death of Corneille Breille, whose macabre end is indirectly foretold by Mackandal's stories of grisly burials (31). More particularly, he remembers a song he used to sing: 'Tambaleándose a la luz de la luna, tomó el camino del regreso, recordando vagamente una canción de otros tiempos, que solía cantar siempre que volvía de la ciudad. Una canción en la que se decían groserías a un rey. Eso era lo importante: *a un rey*' (145). The song has elements of foreboding on both occasions. While the first may be related to the subsequent downfall of the French monarchy, the second forebodes the immediate end of Henri Christophe.

In contrast to the references to monarchy in Parts I and III, Parts II and IV focus on republicanism and the consequences of the overthrow of a monarch. The French Revolution and the Declaration of the Rights of Man, first referred to during the account of Bouckman's conspiracy (78), provide the background to the rebellion and the war of Haitian independence narrated in Part II, which ends with the promise of a republican government. In Part IV, after the interlude of Christophe's reign, republicanism re-emerges with the 'Mulatos Republicanos' (189), thereby completing in the second half of the novel the same movement from monarchy to republic already described in the first half. Parts II and IV both contain a description of those who go into exile to escape the consequences of the fall of monarchy. Part II includes the account of the French refugees who fled from the slave rebellion and endeavoured to recreate in Cuba their former life in Saint-Domingue. Similarly, after the overthrow and death of Christophe, Part IV describes the survivors of his family in Italy who are happy to have found a climate that allows them to live in a manner that reminds them of their former home (171-2). Finally, just as the observations about monarchy associated with Ti Noel in Parts I and III constitute the beginnings of the two cycles, the concluding passages of Parts II and IV indicate their apocalyptic ending and an eventual renewal. The final paragraphs of the last chapter of Part II, significantly titled 'San Trastorno', convey the chaos of Saint-Domingue under the governorship of Rochambeau:

> La partida de Pauline señaló el ocaso de toda sensatez en la colonia. Con el gobierno de Rochambeau los últimos propietarios de la Llanura, perdida la esperanza de volver al bienestar de antaño, se entregaron a una vasta orgía sin coto ni tregua. Nadie hacía caso de los relojes, ni las noches terminaban porque hubiera amanecido. Había que agotar el vino, extenuar la carne, estar de regreso del placer antes de que una catástrofe acabara con una posibilidad de goce. (114)

In spite of the collapse of the social order and the excesses of the war that brings the colonial regime to an end, a new order is announced by the appearance of the negro priests whose prayers are a synthesis of Catholicism and Voodoo (116). The same phenomena of apocalypse and renewal bring the second cycle to a close in the final paragraphs of the novel. The wind that blows from the ocean, destroying everything in its path, comes as if in response to Ti Noel's declaration of war against the Mulatto

Republic and prepares the way for a new order.

The two parallel cycles of events are also supported by the nature and function of some of the characters. Although the narrative is fragmented into four parts, Ti Noel is a means of preserving its continuity. The uniform perspective of a negro slave whose life includes several attempts to win freedom provides a basis for comparing many of the incidents of the novel. However, the presence of other characters and the creation of parallels among them counter-balance his perspective throughout the work. After Ti Noel, Lenormand is the principal figure in the first half. His presence is noticeably limited, however, to Parts I and II. As a white landowner, he represents the dominant class in colonial society, but is not important once Haiti is no longer a colony. He is therefore replaced by others, who represent the changing status of the country. Immediately after the removal of Lenormand, there appear Pauline and Solimán, whose distorted values reflect the period of turmoil during the attempted reconquest of Saint-Domingue by the French. In the later stages of the novel other characters, Christophe, his family, and the mulattoes, are introduced to represent the reinstatement of the standards of colonial times.

Although the replacement of one character by others is a suitable means of confirming the transition from one stage of history to another, the nature of Lenormand and those who replace him indicates that the differences among them are relative. The parallels between Lenormand and the other characters confirm the perpetuation of the same conditions and the repetition of an established cycle. In general terms, all are representative of a decadent class and display either a neglect or a distortion of their own culture. Lenormand strays far from the teaching of Christianity and is an example of the worst in European civilization. Henri Christophe, by building a kingdom in imitation of a European monarchy, disowns the African culture that inspired the struggle for freedom by the slaves and perpetuates the evils against which his people rebelled. Even Solimán's service in the households of Pauline Bonaparte and Henri Christophe indicates a betrayal of his race and religion. In the end, all three, Lenormand, Christophe and Solimán, are victims of their own excesses.

   The parallel between Lenormand and Solimán is taken a step
further than this general similarity. Both are forced to flee from
rebellions that would surely claim their lives. In exile, both lead
a dissipated existence, but seek reconciliation with former beliefs
and the comfort of religion as the moment of death approaches.
Lenormand disavows his association with Freemasonry and
begins to frequent the Cathedral in Santiago de Cuba, while
Solimán, feeling the call of his African homeland, 'trataba de
alcanzar a un Dios que se encontraba en el lejano Dahomey'
(180). The parallel between them also extends to the women
associated with them, both of whom are decidedly histrionic.
Mlle Floridor, Lenormand's third wife, is an unfulfilled actress,
whose frustrated inclination for the stage is inflicted on her
slaves. The adoption of a series of roles is one of the principal
characteristics of Pauline Bonaparte. Her image of herself is initially drawn from literature. Her view of her station as the wife
of General Leclerc, the new Governor of Saint-Domingue, is
derived from the theatre: 'Su amante, el actor Lafont, la había
familiarizado con los papeles de soberana, rugiendo para ella los
versos más reales de *Bayaceto* y de *Mitrídates*' (102). During the
journey to Saint-Domingue and the first months of her stay, her
life is that of a character from a romantic novel (106-7). When
yellow fever breaks out, she changes and adopts the ways of
Solimán. But all these roles are abandoned as she returns to
France. When Solimán again encounters her in Rome it is
through her portrayal as 'Venus Victrix', the goddess of love
carved by the Italian sculptor Antonio Canova. In the light of
Pauline's promiscuous life, the appropriateness of the portrait
requires no comment, but Solimán's encounter with the statue,
which appears to occur after Pauline's death, establishes a
parallel with Lenormand's earlier discovery of his wife's body as
she lay dead in her room in a pose evocative of the suggestive
engraving on her wall (88). Both women are last portrayed, not
as themselves, but in a role that appropriately describes their
character, and both are the cause of a similar hysterical reaction.
Lenormand collapses at the sight of Mlle Floridor, then seizes
his rosary and recites every prayer he can remember. Solimán,

after attempting to massage the statue, just as he massaged Pauline in Saint-Domingue, runs amok and calls upon the gods of his African homeland.

In addition to confirming the structure of the text as two parallel sequences, the introduction of figures with similar characteristics and functions also gives the reader the sensation that all that occurs is foreshadowed or has already occurred in a different form. This sensation is equally enhanced by in-numerable allusions or cross-references within the text whereby actions are repeated, anticipated, or referred to again after they have already been narrated. After Bouckman's execution, his head is displayed in exactly the same spot where Mackandal was burned alive (88). Lenormand marries not once, but three times, and just as his second wife sermonized the slaves, his third appears to exemplify the very sins against which she preached (75-6). The longing that Lenormand feels for France is counter-balanced by his yearning for the colony after he has been in Europe for a while (73). Pauline's voyage from France to Saint-Domingue is paralleled by her return journey and the two occasions are linked by the similarity of her conduct on board the ships that carry her. Mackandal's return, four years after the failure of his campaign against the colonists, is expected by his followers and his leadership anticipates the eventual role of Bouckman (56). The dogs used by the French as one of the last desperate measures to suppress the uprising recall earlier references to their use in the hunt for Mackandal (41 and 53). Similarly, although Corneille Breille and Henri Christophe do not play a significant role until Part III, their appearance has already been anticipated. Breille is referred to in passing in the first chapter (30), while Christophe is mentioned twice in Part II (72 and 92), both times in connection with his ownership of La Corona. By contrast, the appearance of Solimán and Pauline Bonaparte in Part II is not anticipated. But the episodes con-cerned with their association are recalled and re-enacted in Part IV through Solimán's encounter with Canova's statue in the Borghese Palace. Recovery of the past occurs more frequently, however, through Ti Noel's memory. This tendency begins in the first chapter, when he recalls the stories (27) told to him by

Mackandal even before Mackandal himself has appeared in the novel. Later, after Mackandal's death, the legend that has grown around him is frequently remembered (76, 99, 123, for example). Ti Noel's movements also lead to a recovery of the past. Each time he returns to Cap Français (72-3, 141-5) or to Lenormand's former estate (123-4, 140, 181), earlier times are recalled and related to the present. Finally, his review of the outstanding events of his life in the last pages of the novel amounts to a recovery of the entire text.

On the basis of the preceding description of the organization of the content in *El reino de este mundo*, it is evident that the cyclical structures of the novel have several forms. It would be incorrect to consider the work exclusively in the terms of one of them and to focus, for example, solely on the four cycles based on the four parts of the narrative, on the two parallel cycles derived from the similarity of events narrated in the two halves of the novel, or on a series of more random repetitions and allusions. These structures are all related manifestations of a single phenomenon. The content of the novel is either drawn from history or, in the case of its fictional elements, carefully inserted into an historical context and made to appear authentic. However, the relations among events or characters are derived less from history than from Carpentier's arrangement and description of them in the text. Thus, the circular patterns, achieved through various forms of repetition and parallel, produce a novel in which all incidents are carefully integrated, and contribute to an interpretation of history that is particular to the text. Although the linear development of the plot and the quest for freedom exemplified by the life of Ti Noel and his experience of a number of revolutionary movements represent a linear progression from the past to the present, the past is never totally left behind. The constant repetitions and parallels in the text convey the idea that each new development entails a recovery of the past. The conventional view of history as a chain of consecutive events is thereby replaced by a view in which history, while continually advancing in accordance with the passage of time, also turns back on itself, as if following the trajectory of a spiral. In these circumstances, an objective, historical chronology loses its importance as a basis of interpretation. It is less important to know how events are chronologically related than to realize that each series of incidents incorporates and repeats the past. The evident connection between the novel and its historical sources is relevant because it tells us much about the process of composition and is a means of authenticating the content of the novel, but the interpretation of the content itself must be derived from its organization in the text.

The Sources of Conflict

The different cycles in *El reino de este mundo* are united by the presence of Ti Noel, whose continuous quest for freedom emphasizes that the rebellions described in the text are initiated by a single group of people always in pursuit of the same goal. All the rebellions are directed against the same evil, slavery and its equivalent, forced labour. The terms 'esclavo' and 'amo' appear on the first page of the novel and are used repeatedly in Parts I and II. More than anything else, it is the reinstitution of the slave-master relationship that confounds Ti Noel when he returns to Haiti from Cuba and discovers the kingdom of Henri Christophe. The relationship also recurs after Christophe's downfall and the arrival of the 'agrimensores': 'Ti Noel supo, por un fugitivo, que las tareas agrícolas se habían vuelto obligatorias y que el látigo estaba ahora en manos de Mulatos Republicanos, nuevos amos de la Llanura del Norte' (189). The term 'amos', used again (197) when Ti Noel finally calls for a rebellion against the mulattoes, places them in the same category as the French colonists who originally brought the negroes to Haiti as slaves. If the latter always struggle against the same evil, it is because they are always oppressed by the same class of people, who belong to a different race and occupy a superior position in the social order. The white settlers are a class of landowners who maintain their privileged status for as long as they have greater strength. Allowing for obvious differences, Christophe ultimately belongs to the same class. Although historians have not been able to determine his background conclusively, he was born not in Saint-Domingue, but in another Caribbean colony, possibly Grenada or St Kitts, and was of mixed racial origin. No reference is made to this in the novel, but he is evidently not of the same class as the negroes of Haiti. The two references in the novel to the period before he came to power allude to his status as a property owner (72 and 92). By the same standards, the 'Mulatos Republicanos' are a class apart from the negro majority. Even in colonial times they were a caste superior to the negro slaves (84), and when they take control of Northern Haiti after the fall of Christophe they are clearly associated with ownership of the land. If the differences among the colonists, Christophe, and the mulattoes are eliminated on the grounds that they all represent the same social class, none of the uprisings of the slaves, before or after gaining statutory freedom, can be considered as successful. The need for constant revolution, therefore, arises not because earlier movements turned sour, but because they never achieved their objective. Since power is always retained by a hierarchically superior class the slaves never gain control of their own lives.

The preceding comments permit the underlying nature of the cyclical structures in *El reino de este mundo* to be identified more clearly. Class conflict is the force that causes events to repeat themselves. Each of the rebellions described in the novel is one of the periodic clashes that erupt in a society existing in a state of perpetual tension as a result of the conflicting elements it contains. Undoubtedly, the conditions described by Carpentier are particularly relevant to Haiti, but the overall pattern of cyclical repetition has certain universal implications. The justification for considering Haiti as a universal paradigm is founded in part on the existence of comparable circumstances in other environments, especially in Latin America. But it is also derived from the way in which Haiti is described in the novel. The text conveys the conditions of conflict in all their complexity. Race, culture, politics, and economics are all presented as interrelated sources of the same problem. At the same time, the conclusion of the novel provides an explanation of the situation in Haiti that is universally applicable. Ti Noel's metamorphoses suggest that the existence of a constant state of tension in society is a natural phenomenon. When he lives as an ant, his experiences are comparable to those he endured in human form

(191). As a goose, he is an outcast, totally unable to penetrate the group:

> El clan aparecía ahora como una comunidad aristocrática, absolutamente cerrada a todo individuo de otra casta. El Gran Ansar de Sans-Souci no hubiera querido el menor trato con el Gran Ansar de Dondón. De haberse encontrado frente a frente, hubiera estallado una guerra. Por ello Ti Noel comprendió pronto que, aunque insistiera durante años, jamás tendría el menor acceso a las funciones y ritos del clan. Se le había dado a entender claramente que no le bastaba ser ganso para creerse que todos los gansos fueran iguales. Ningún ganso conocido había cantado ni bailado el día de sus bodas. Nadie, de los vivos, lo había visto nacer. Se presentaba, sin el menor expediente de limpieza de sangre, ante cuatro generaciones en palmas. En suma, era un meteco. (195-6)

The social structure and its tensions are biologically determined. As a result, society is divided into impenetrable units that conflict with each other at the slightest provocation.

Although the biological source of social tension is not described so explicitly until the end of the novel, the idea that conflict is caused by fundamental differences of a comparable nature appears in the first pages of the text. Ti Noel's reflections on the prints outside the bookseller's in Cap Français provide a clear description of the two opposing groups:

> En el Africa, el rey era guerrero, cazador, juez y sacerdote; su simiente preciosa engrosaba, en centenares de vientres, una vigorosa estirpe de héroes. En Francia, en España, en cambio, el rey enviaba sus generales a combatir; era incompetente para dirimir litigios, se hacía regañar por cualquier fraile confesor, y, en cuanto, a riñones, no pasaba de engendrar un príncipe debilucho, incapaz de acabar con un venado sin ayuda de sus monteros, al que designaban, con inconsciente ironía, por el nombre de un pez tan inofensivo y frívolo como era el delfín. Allá, en cambio —en *Gran*

Allá—, había príncipes duros como el yunque, y príncipes
que eran el leopardo, y príncipes que conocían el lenguaje
de los árboles, y príncipes que mandaban sobre los cuatro
puntos cardinales, dueños de la nube, de la semilla, del
bronce y del fuego. (28-9)

The strength and vitality of the Africans stand in marked contrast to the debility and decadence of the Europeans,
establishing the basis of the opposition elaborated in more detail
in the course of the text and used as one of the central elements
of all the major incidents narrated.

Egoism is one of the most noticeable characteristics of the
Europeans and is attributed to both Lenormand and Pauline.
One of the first descriptions of Lenormand, his visit to a barber,
shows his attention to personal grooming and directly associates
him with the periwigged courtiers of France portrayed in the
prints. Pauline's concern for her appearance is elaborated a little
more extensively and is reflected both in her evident interest in
clothes (103) and in the image of herself that she consciously
cultivates from her reading of popular works of literature
(102-7). This self-centredness is just as apparent in the personal
relationships established by both characters. As a landowner,
Lenormand treats his slaves simply as a source of wealth. This is
the only reason why Ti Noel and a dozen others are spared from
slaughter after Bouckman's rebellion (89). By the same token,
Pauline's association with Solimán is entirely selfish and assists
her in confirming her own image of herself. The text leaves little
doubt about the promiscuity of both Lenormand and Pauline.
In the case of the former, in particular, the text refers to his
three marriages and numerous extra-marital relations both in
Saint-Domingue and Cuba, but contains no reference to any
children. The omission suitably emphasizes the sterility of the
social class represented by Lenormand and places him in the
same category as the European kings imagined by Ti Noel at the
beginning of the novel.

The weakness of individuals is comparable to the state of their
culture. In spite of the material progress of Cap Français,
described in the first chapter of Part II, the account of life in

Lenormand's household that immediately follows it in the text reveals the moral decline of the colony. Religion is not a source of cultural strength or a real guide to its followers. It is turned to, somewhat ineffectively, only in moments of crisis, as when Lenormand discovers the body of Mlle Floridor or realizes that he is old and approaching death himself. The function of religion, although not referred to extensively, has become distorted. Lenormand's second marriage was arranged ('alcahueteado', 59) by the parish priest, and his second wife is a 'beata', who uses religion to repress the slaves (59, 75). Above all, European culture has lost its spontaneity and become inflexible. Like the Europeans described in the novel, it is self-centred. In times of calamity, it does not have the resilience to provide either consolation or remedy. When yellow fever breaks out, Pauline rapidly loses all confidence in her own doctors and turns to Solimán. When the slaves use poison against their masters under the direction of Mackandal, Lenormand and his kind are totally perplexed. In desperation, unable to discover either the source or nature of the poison, they resort to barbarism (50-1). The hermetic nature of their culture is most clearly shown by its inability to convey anything but a distorted view of reality. In Pauline's case, this is emphasized by the false ideas derived from her reading, but even those who have lived longer in the colony are no less deceived. They do not suspect the existence or vitality of the cultural bonds among the negro slaves. The point is made most clearly through the two versions of Mackandal's execution and Lenormand's reaction to his own mistaken interpretation of the incident: 'comentaba con su beata esposa la insensibilidad de los negros ante el suplicio de un semejante —sacando de ello ciertas consideraciones filosóficas sobre la desigualdad de las razas humanas, que se proponía desarrollar en un discurso colmado de citas latinas' (67). It is only after the general uprising of the slaves, when it is too late, that they achieve a greater awareness of reality. But even then, the egoism of the colonists and their error in overlooking the importance of the practices and beliefs of their slaves are countered by a rhetorical question: '¿Pero acaso una persona culta podía haberse preocupado por las salvajes creencias de gentes que adoraban una serpiente?' (91).

The non-Europeans who have adopted European ways are equally decadent. Solimán is not an authentic representative of his people. Both before and during the epidemic of yellow fever he behaves as a willing accomplice to Pauline's fantasies. Unlike the slaves in general, for whom Voodoo is a source of strength and liberation, Solimán turns it into a mere exhibition of superstitious folklore. The completeness of Solimán's betrayal of his culture is confirmed once more by his service under Christophe, who is as unauthentic as he, and, again, by his life in Rome, where he falls prey to alcohol and willingly exploits the interest he excites as an object of curiosity (173-4). The emptiness of his existence is revealed when he encounteres the statue of Pauline in the Borghese Palace. Although the statue makes him recall the sensuality of his former relationship with Pauline, real life eludes him. Both the statue and Pauline are dead and the Borghese Palace itself is little more than a dusty mausoleum. While Solimán's reaction to the statue may remind us of the classical story of Pygmalion, the outcome of his apparent attempt to bring it to life seems to indicate the ossification of European culture. Unlike the Voodoo belief in animism, European mythology has lost its vitality and is reduced to a mere collection of stories. In the light of his experience, Solimán's behaviour is almost predictable. He appears to become aware of the implications of what he is doing and realizes the emptiness of the culture he has adopted. When he lies on his sickbed, presumably dying of malaria contracted in Rome, he longs to return to the Caribbean and to regain the culture he has forsaken.

Henri Christophe, the second of the non-Europeans to adopt European ways, is also characterized by egoism and a sense of regret at not having attached more importance to the culture of his own people (157-8). His attention to appearances and adoption of European culture are plainly reflected in the style of his court (125-9). His egoism is evident in the use of the resources of his kingdom for the construction of a citadel intended for his own aggrandizement and security. Symbolically, it will never be completed and will serve only as his own tomb. The vanity of his achievements is clearly shown when he is alone in his palace after his guards and all but a few retainers have left him. The adornments of his palace and the titles he has given himself mean nothing. At the end, he has only the echo of his own footsteps and his own image reflected in the mirrors on the walls of his court (156-9). He has become a monarch in the style of Europe, much like the King of France portrayed in the prints described at the beginning of the novel. His son is known as 'el Delfín' (171) and he is prey to the murmurings of a priest (144). Moreover, like Solimán, Christophe realizes the weakness of the culture he has adopted: 'Ahora comprendía que los verdaderos traidores a su causa, aquella noche, eran San Pedro con su llave, los capuchinos de San Francisco y el negro San Benito, con la Virgen de semblante oscuro y manto azul, y los Evangelistas, cuyos libros había hecho besar en cada juramento de fidelidad' (161).

The 'Mulatos Republicanos' introduced in the final chapters of the novel will presumably follow a path similar to that of Christophe, for they too appear to have adopted European ways. The mulatto women, referred to in the first chapter (30), already show a love of European fashion and display before the Europeans are driven from the colony. The mulattoes who appear at the end of the novel are also dressed in a style that shows European influence (188) and behave in a way that recalls the barbarism of the European colonists.

In contrast to the characters associated with European culture, those who remain faithful to their African heritage are strong and vital. The virility of Ti Noel, implied in the first sentence of the novel by his association with the choice of a studhorse for Lenormand, is referred to explicitly in the final sentence of Part I. The night of the execution of Mackandal 'Ti Noel embarazó de jimaguas a una de las fámulas de cocina, trabándola, por tres veces, dentro de uno de los pesebres de la caballeriza' (67). This, of course, is in contrast to Lenormand's decision to write an essay full of Latin quotations. Indeed, in contrast to the sterility of Lenormand, Ti Noel is prolific. At the beginning of Part II, he is described as having fathered twelve children by one of Lenormand's cooks (74). When Mackandal is first introduced, his masculinity is also emphasized: 'Era fama que su voz grave y sorda le conseguía todo de las negras. Y que sus artes de narrador, caracterizando los personajes con muecas terribles, imponían el silencio a los hombres' (33). It is referred to again shortly before his reappearance after four years of absence: 'Mackandal había cerrado el ciclo de sus metamorfosis, volviendo a asentarse, nervudo y duro, con testículos como piedras, sobre sus piernas de hombre' (57). As men with strong personalities, the negroes have qualities of leadership that are lacking in the white settlers. Such qualities, evident in Mackandal and Bouckman, who readily command a large and faithful following, are also found in Ti Noel. In the last chapters of the novel, he is described as a patriarch in his domain. In spite of his advanced age and apparent senility, he is treated with respect and reverence. His rule is peaceful and benign. He is also aware, however vaguely, that he has a mission to accomplish (183) and when the moment arrives is ready to place himself at the head of his people, much like Mackandal and Bouckman before him, to urge them to declare war against the new masters.

The vitality of the principal negro characters in the novel owes much to their culture. Although they are removed from their homeland, their culture is still part of them. It is kept alive by associating their actions with the deities of their African past and by passing their heritage to future generations, as when Ti Noel tells the stories of Mackandal to his children. In contrast to the artificiality of European culture, the strength of African culture is its authenticity and association with the natural world. Mackandal's power is his understanding of nature. His capacity to use it and harmonize with it are clear from his ability to find a poison to combat the white settlers and from the power of lycanthropy attributed to him by his followers. In Parts III and IV of the novel, Ti Noel has acquired similar attributes. Even before his power of lycanthropy is demonstrated in the final pages of the novel, he has learned to communicate with nature: 'Ti Noel nunca estaba solo aunque estuviese solo. Desde hacía mucho tiempo había adquirido el arte de conversar con las sillas, las ollas, o bien con una vaca, una guitarra, o con su propia sombra' (120). Above all, the blacks of Haiti draw strength from their religion and confidence from their gods, who are referred to in the novel at all its significant moments: when Mackandal's return is anticipated (56); when his metamorphosis apparently saves him from the fire (66-7); during the conspiracy led by Bouckman (78-9); in the war of independence against the French (115-16); on Ti Noel's return to Haiti from Cuba (121-2); and through the sound of the drums heard during the revolt against Christophe (159-60). It is this vitality that distinguishes the beliefs of the negroes from those of the Europeans. Unlike the myths of Europe, which are no longer able to influence the course of history, those of the New World Africans are still alive and retain their power to move.

At the risk of oversimplifying such a complex novel as *El reino de este mundo* the preceding discussion justifies the conclusion that its central issue is the conflict between a dynamic culture and another in a state of decay. While the structure of the plot and the elaboration of the characters both point to this interpretation, the cyclical repetition of events and the continual antagonism of the same forces confirm that the conflict is not a fleeting phenomenon, but part of a process unfolding over an extended period of time. Carpentier's account of the process, however, although conveyed through a work of fiction, is not given in abstract terms. The decadent culture is European and is represented principally by France. Its antagonist is American and is represented by the dynamic culture of the New World Africans. In these circumstances, even while respecting the independence of the text from its sources, the reader cannot refrain from invoking his own knowledge of the world and searching for a frame of reference in which to place an understanding of the two antagonists and their conflict.

In searching for an appropriate frame of reference, some attention must be given to that provided by Carpentier in the prologue. The opposition he establishes between Surrealism and 'lo real maravilloso' is founded on considerations similar to those that underly the opposition between the two cultures described in the novel. Carpentier claims that a sense of the marvellous obtained through the techniques of Surrealism is artificially contrived. It lacks the conviction, spontaneity, and vitality he attributes to 'lo real maravilloso' and considers as qualities of the history of America. In spite of this parallel, however, there is a significant difference of scale between the opinions advanced in the prologue and those implied by the novel. Carpentier's distrust of Surrealism does not appear to provide sufficient grounds for a broader criticism of European culture that implies a more general state of decadence and includes periods of history earlier than Surrealism. If both the novel and the prologue are accepted as arguments in favour of the same idea, it is clear that neither of them conveys Carpentier's thought completely.

During the years of his association with the avant-garde of the 1920s and 30s, Carpentier also came into contact with ideas concerning the nature of history which significantly affected his view of the relation between Latin America and Europe. Among the most influential were those of Oswald Spengler (1880-1936), elaborated in *The Decline of the West* (*Der Untergang des Abendlandes*), the two volumes of which were published in 1918 and 1922. Spengler's theories spread widely and quickly. In 1923 the important Spanish periodical *Revista de Occidente* carried an introduction to Spengler entitled 'Una nueva filosofía de la historia: ¿Europa en decadencia?', and, in the following year, published a chapter from the third volume of the Spanish translation of *The Decline of the West*. Spengler's attempt to identify and apply invariable laws governing the rise and fall of civilizations was not a new undertaking among philosophers of history, but the timing of the publication of his work, shortly after the end of the First World War, virtually ensured an immediate impact. According to the scheme he proposed, Europe had already entered a period of decline and was destined to lose its cultural hegemony. Although he was criticized as unscholarly, the popularity of some of his more pessimistic predictions was undoubtedly fostered by the climate of the times, particularly as the First World War was followed by the Depression, the rise of Fascism, and a second global conflict. For Latin America, however, *The Decline of the West* was a source of hope. As Roberto González Echevarría shows in his discussion of the importance of Spengler in the development of Carpentier's thought, the salvation of America was linked to the predicament of Europe:

> Spengler offers a view of universal history in which there is
> no fixed center, and where Europe is simply one more
> culture. From this arises a relativism in morals and values:
> no more acculturation of blacks, no need to absorb
> European civilization. Spengler provided the philosophical
> ground on which to stake the autonomy of Latin American
> culture and deny its filial relation to Europe. Spengler's
> cyclic conception of the history of cultures kindled the
> hope that if Europe was in decline, Latin America must be
> then in an earlier, more promising stage of her own in-
> dependent evolution. (*8*, p.56)

When set against this background, the opposition between
Europe and America described in *El reino de este mundo*,
although placed in an historical context, acquires greater im-
mediacy and can be reconciled with the different orientation of
Carpentier's criticism of European culture in the prologue. The
novel is set principally during the French Revolution and the
Napoleonic Era, the same period identified by Spengler as the
beginning of European decline. When referring to Surrealism in
the prologue, Carpentier simply described a later stage of the
same process of decay. By resorting to history as the subject of
the novel, he was not therefore solely distancing himself from
his own experiences and using the past as an analogy for the present. Just as his recourse to the past transcends the mere anecdotal recording of events, it also reveals his interest in history as
a process to which both past and present belong.

Carpentier's acceptance of Spengler's doctrine of European
decline as a valid description of this process is confirmed by a
series of six articles published in the Cuban periodical *Carteles* in
November and December 1941. Echoing Spengler's work,
Carpentier discussed the state of European culture under the
general title 'El ocaso de Europa'. Although provoked by the
plight of wartime Europe, his commentary includes a particularly biting denunciation of France that attributes its downfall to
the stagnation and decadence of its culture. Emphasizing the

United States as much as any of the Latin countries and referring to advanced rather than to primitive cultures, he claims that the future belongs to America: '¡Hace tiempo ya que la antorcha de la civilización ha pasado, de manos del viejo corredor exhausto, a las del juvenil y atlético campeón!' Moreover, his point is made through direct reference to Spengler: 'Spengler dijo cierta vez que ningún esfuerzo humano podía hacer que un árbol, llegado al ocaso de su existencia, reverdeciera una vez más... Las naciones no son gatos de siete vidas. Civilizaciones de bastante más importancia histórica que la francesa o la alemana han durado, en suma, bastante menos que estas últimas' (*Carteles*, 16 November 1941, p.75).

Whether through *The Decline of the West* or popularizations of its theories, Carpentier's contact with Spengler's analysis certainly accounts for the stark distinction between European decadence and American vitality in *El reino de este mundo*. For Carpentier and others of his generation, Spengler provided a basis for interpreting the times. In the case of Carpentier, it gave him a point from which to focus on the various elements of his own experience and to see from a common perspective his association with the avant-garde in Cuba and France, his reading of Spanish American history, his rediscovery of America on returning to Cuba in 1939, and his visit to Haiti in 1943. Much of what Spengler wrote, however, synthesized and reformulated ideas that had already circulated for some time. Although Spengler fully acknowledged his debt only to Nietzsche (1844-1900) and Goethe (1749-1832), his work must also be considered in the light of that of several others: Vico (1668-1744), Hegel (1770-1831), Burckhardt (1818-97), Marx (1818-83), Sorel (1847-1922), Pareto (1848-1923), and Bergson (1859-1941), for example. The work of these men led in different directions and to different conclusions, but they shared a number of general preoccupations, among which were the nature of history and its cyclical character, the structure of society and the rise and fall of governments and civilizations, the role of barbarism and art, and the function of the irrational in determining the march of history. Carpentier could have assimilated the principal concepts developed by any of these writers without having read their work directly. Their ideas were already part of the intellectual climate of Carpentier's age and he would have made contact with them from a variety of sources. Although the general thrust and organization of his own thought at the time he was writing *El reino de este mundo* was undoubtedly oriented by Spengler, there is much in his writing that may be traced to other sources.

The relation of Carpentier to Giambattista Vico is a particularly interesting example. The first edition of Vico's *New Science* (*Scienza nuova*) was published in 1725. A second edition appeared in 1730 and a much revised third edition was published shortly after his death in 1744. Although not widely read before the nineteenth century, his work gradually won increased attention outside Italy and is now considered an important precursor of the modern human sciences. A connection between Carpentier and Vico is referred to by González Echevarría, who suggests that in the Cuban author's later fiction 'Vico has come to replace Spengler as a philosophical underpinning' (*8*, p.259). The points of contact he identifies are the anti-Cartesian stance of *El recurso del método* (1974)[7] and the idea of historical recurrence (Vico's 'ricorso') in *Los advertidos*, a short story by Carpentier of the 1960s which uses the theme of the Flood to focus on the opportunity given to Man to begin anew and remake history. Without entering into a discussion of the later fiction, it is interesting to note that there is much in Vico to illuminate Carpentier's earlier work.

An anti-Cartesian stance is not explicity elaborated in *El reino de este mundo*. But by showing how the history of Haiti, in the Age of Reason, is determined by myth and religion, the novel illustrates the importance of irrational forces in shaping history. This stance, in addition to the implied rejection of a means of understanding America through a philosophy that originated in Europe, is compatible with Vico's writings. Vico's understanding of the history of nations in the light of their spiritual needs and desires sets him apart from his contemporaries of the eight-

---

[7] The term implies rejection of René Descartes (1596-1650), whose advocacy of the supremacy of reason is subordinated to the notion that irrational forces in the human spirit determine the course of history.

eenth century who generally adhered to the principles of Cartesian rationalism. Carpentier's account of the history of Haiti is clearly based on a similar stand. Whether or not he derived it from Vico, of course, is a different matter. However, given Carpentier's meticulous use of sources, it would have been consistent with his approach for him to have consulted the work of the philosophers of the age about which he was writing and to have found in Vico a writer who had become more respectable in Carpentier's own time and who advocated views he could easily share.

The similarity with Vico is not solely a matter of philosophical orientation. He argued that the history of nations passes through three stages. The last of them, called the age of humans to indicate Man's greater understanding of the true nature of things, is represented in the novel by the Europeans. In Vico's scheme, just as in Spengler's, Carpentier's description would place them in a period of decadence and approaching barbarism. By contrast, the Africans of the New World in *El reino de este mundo* have many of the characteristics attributed by Vico to earlier stages of development. The implications of the African past, Voodoo, and the story of Mackandal are indications of the divine or poetic age, in which Man's imagination served him to create a religion describing his view of the world and his relation to his surroundings and the divine. The later chapters of the novel establish a further link with Vico by indicating a culmination of the first age and passage into the second, the age of heroes. In this age, both in imitation of divine structures and as a means of self-preservation, social organization was founded on the family or the clan. The description of Ti Noel's situation at the end of the novel implies that his society has reached that stage. As a believer in the myths of the past, a follower of Mackandal, and a participant in the history of his people, he becomes a hero who finally leads the fight against the new masters. Not only is he a patriarch in his own kingdom, the head of the clan, as described in the chapter 'La real casa', but his metamorphosis persuades him that the clan is the basis of the political structure of the world to which he belongs.

The mechanism identified by Vico as the cause of change is

'ricorso'. It implies a process of recurrence or renewal that occurs in nations and civilizations either at the end of each age, as societies relapse into barbarism, or at intervals during the course of each age itself. The principle of 'ricorso' does not entail exact repetition. It proposes that history is characterized by advances which are also a return to the past brought about by the periodic endeavour among nations to recapture their original spirit and strength. Once they have embarked upon their course through history, however, each return is undertaken reflexively as a result of the memory and experience acquired by Man and the sense of his own becoming that he has developed. The form of recurrence that underlies the cyclical repetitions described in *El reino de este mundo* is of the same nature. Each rebellion is a conscious endeavour to return to the spirit of the African past, which is introduced at the beginning of the novel in the description of the African monarch and is repeatedly referred to throughout the text. The life of Ti Noel is particularly important in this respect. His return to Haiti after a period of exile in Cuba is a literal and figurative recovery of the past. Before his illusions are broken by his discovery of the true nature of conditions under Christophe's rule, he rejoices at recovering the land and the spirit of the Great Pact (121-2), believing that he has regained both the mythic past of Africa and its historical continuation in the New World represented by the freedom won through Bouckman's rebellion. The final call to arms and the conclusion of the novel are more fully indicative of the reflexiveness of Ti Noel's return to the past and the sense of history conveyed by the text. The reflexiveness of his actions is underlined by the understanding of Mackandal he finally achieves and by the knowledge of human society he gains through lycanthropy. Ti Noel's epiphany is the moment of lucidity he experiences before his end (196-7). In the light of the past and his own life, he realizes that the sense of man's own becoming is the control he takes of his own history by imposing tasks on himself in an endeavour to improve. The apocalyptic end, the disappearance of Ti Noel, and the buffeting of the landscape by the elements simply indicate a new beginning, another 'ricorso'.

Regardless of the parallels, the relation between Carpentier and Vico is only tentatively proposed. The presence of many writers is felt in Carpentier's work and the true extent of his indebtedness to them, both in *El reino de este mundo* and in his later fiction, still needs to be studied more fully. Of the group mentioned above, for instance, the majority are anti-Cartesian in the sense that they adopt a method of intuitive comparison and stress the spirit of history. Vico simply did it earlier. Instead of the ideas of Vico, the novel might also be examined for its relation to Marxist economic history or to Pareto's view of political history as the history of social elites. Without belittling the importance of Spengler, *El reino de este mundo* reflects the intellectual eclecticism of Carpentier's formation and the climate of thought in which he lived. On this basis, any comprehensive interpretation of the novel must necessarily be broad. It is evidently not just a fictional history of Haiti, nor even solely an attempt to find a new rationale from which to argue in favour of the cultural autonomy and respectability of Latin America, although both these themes are important to the general meaning of the text. The novel is to be interpreted at many levels, but at its most profound it is an endeavour to understand and explain the wider currents of history, and it is to this end that the structure of its content is directed.

5. Narrative Technique and Style

Narration

In addition to characterization and plot, the novelist has other means of addressing the reader, among which a narrator is one of the most important. Modern literary criticism has established that the author and the narrator should not be confused.[8] Although the voice of the narrator is often assumed by an author and, in this sense, may be his mouthpiece, the narrator itself is a fictive entity to which the discourse reproduced as the text is attributed. Just as the discourse itself is imaginary, so is the person who utters it. These distinctions are clearly evident in *El reino de este mundo*. Although written in the twentieth century, it describes events belonging to the eighteenth and nineteenth. This fact alone immediately dissociates the author from the narrator. Regardless of Carpentier's familiarity with history, he did not witness any of the historical events and did not know any of the characters described in the novel. He is therefore able to narrate the story only if he imagines himself to be someone with a knowledge he does not actually possess. The fictional parts of the novel are, of course, imaginary and have no real witness, not even Carpentier, who can only imagine that he has seen them. In this sense, neither the historical nor the fictional elements of the narrative belong to the discourse of the real Carpentier. They are told by Carpentier, not as himself, but as a narrator, as if he were an actor playing a role. Or they are told by another being, a fictive narrator, whose existence is implied by the existence of the text and who is created as a witness capable of telling what is contained in the narrative. In either

---

[8] Discussion of the narrator and use of the term focalization later in this section are drawn principally from Gérard Genette, *Narrative Discourse: An Essay in Method*, translated by Jane E. Lewin, with a foreword by Jonathan Culler (Ithaca: Cornell University Press, 1980), pp.161-262. By focalization, I mean restriction of what the reader is presumed to perceive at any given moment to what is seen by the narrator or by a character.

case, a game is evidently being played in which the reader agrees to follow the discourse attributed to an imaginary speaker. In the light of these considerations, it is relevant to ask who tells the story in *El reino de este mundo*, what the characteristics of this person are, and what effect his presence has on the message conveyed to the reader.

As the only character whose existence spans the entire period of time that elapses in the novel and who witnesses several of the major incidents of the plot, Ti Noel is a useful point of reference in the organization of the narrative and an important source of its unity. However, he is not the narrator and events are not seen through his eyes only. The narrator is not identified with any of the characters in the novel. He is an undramatized figure, never directly introduced to the reader but responsible for telling a story from which he is absent. Paradoxically, his absence allows him greater freedom and mobility. Were he a dramatized figure, he would be limited by his particular identity and would be able to give a reliable account only of what he saw or was told as a character in the novel. In fact, the narrator has a full view of all events. His ubiquity allows him to follow the characters wherever they go and his ability to see what takes place in Haiti, Santiago de Cuba, Rome, or on board Leclerc's flagship in mid-Atlantic is accepted without question, Similarly, the narrator is not bound by conventional chronology, but can change the order of events. The episodes concerning Pauline's visit to Saint-Domingue are told as a flashback which disrupts the chronological sequence. But they are not inserted in the text by a different narrator, who tells them as if they were a memory recalled by one character to another. Before these episodes begin, the narrator mentions the news of Saint-Domingue heard by Ti Noel from some negroes newly arrived in Santiago (101-2). Presumably it deals with the French invasion. But the version given to the reader contains information concerning the life of Pauline Bonaparte that is beyond the possible knowledge of a negro slave and is therefore not the same version heard by Ti Noel. The reference to the news heard by Ti Noel is simply a mechanism adopted by the narrator to prepare the reader for an evident break in chronology.

El reino de este mundo, then, is told by a single anonymous voice (assumed to be Carpentier's if the reader wishes) whose knowledge of events is complete and authoritative. His reliability as an interpreter of the world described in the novel is established in part by the absence of a contradictory voice and, in part, by his anonymity and ability to describe objectively. In the following two passages, for instance, the scene is focalized (see note 8) by the narrator, and the only evident subjective element is his choice of what is included:

> En una esquina bailaban los títeres de un bululú. Más adelante, un marinero ofrecía a las damas un monito del Brasil, vestido a la española. En las tabernas se descorchaban botellas de vino, refrescadas en barriles de sal y de arena mojada. El padre Cornejo, cura de Limonade, acababa de llegar a la Parroquial Mayor, montado en su mula de color burro. (30)
>
> Asiendo un cuchillo, Ti Noel cortó las correas que sujetaban el caballo al mástil del trapiche. Los esclavos de la tenería invadieron el molino, corriendo detrás del amo. También llegaban los trabajadores del bucán y del secadero de cacao. Ahora, Mackandal tiraba de su brazo triturado, haciendo girar los cilindros en sentido contrario. (35)

Since many passages are narrated this way, scenes and events are often described with a kind of photographic realism in which the obvious intervention of a subjective viewer is lacking. But the narrator does not always adopt the stance of a non-partisan observer. Much of the text is coloured by a negative evaluation of the European and Europeanized characters and a positive evaluation of the negroes implied by the consistent description of the former as decadent and the latter as culturally dynamic. Through direct statements and implied comparisons, the narrator's opinion is therefore constantly felt. The description of Lenormand's household during the heyday of the colony in 'La hija de Minos y de Pasifae', the life of the exiles in Cuba in 'Cuba de Santiago', the chapters concerned with Henri

Christophe in Part III, and the account of Solimán's life in Rome clearly illustrate the point. In 'La hija de Minos y de Pasifae', for example, the narrator leaves no doubt about his opinion of Mlle Floridor and Lenormand:

> Sin embargo, con la edad, Monsieur Lenormand de Mezy se había vuelto maniático y borracho. Una erotomanía perpetua le tenía acechando, a todas horas, a las esclavas adolescentes cuyo pigmento lo excitaba por el olfato. Era cada vez más aficionado a imponer castigos corporales a los hombres, sobre todo cuando los sorprendía fornicando fuera del matrimonio. Por su parte, ajada y mordida por el paludismo, la cómica se vengaba de su fracaso artístico haciendo azotar por cualquier motivo a las negras que la bañaban y peinaban. Ciertas noches se daba a beber. No era raro entonces que hiciera levantar la dotación entera, alta ya la luna, para declamar ante los esclavos, entre eructos de malvasía, los grandes papeles que nunca había alcanzado a interpretar. (74-5)

By contrast, references to Ti Noel's numerous offspring (74) and the stories he tells them about Mackandal and their African heritage (76) convey the dynamism and vitality of the negro.

Since the novel contains no narrative voice other than that of a single narrator, his partisan stance is unchallenged as the sole reliable source of interpretation of events. The primacy of his interpretation is maintained by the control he exerts on the narrative and his assimilation of other perspectives both to his own view of the world and his own discourse. Just as the narrator has an uninhibited view of external reality, he also sees how reality is internalized by the characters. Although they are focalized by the narrator as part of the world described by him, they are used as secondary focalizers when their own thoughts and feelings are conveyed:

> Pauline se había sentido un poco reina a bordo de aquella fragata... (102)
> Pauline recordaba vagamente algo del *Helesponto blan-*

> *queando bajo nuestros remos...* (102)
> Sabía que cuando los faroles se mecían en lo alto de los mástiles... (103)
> Seguía enterneciéndose con *Un negro como hay pocos blancos*, la lacrimosa novela de Joseph Lavalée, y gozando despreocupadamente de aquel lujo, de aquella abundancia que nunca había conocido en su niñez... (106)
> ...creyéndose un poco Virginia, un poco Atala... (107)

The preceding phrases, all from the first of the chapters concerned with Pauline's visit to Saint-Domingue, each contain a main verb that describes an interior action. Although the narrative voice is still that of the primary narrator, it does not convey his view of Pauline exclusively. The verbs expressing thought and feeling indicate that Pauline and her surroundings are focalized by Pauline herself. Similar effects are obtained through verbs of seeing, as in the account of Ti Noel's discoveries on returning to Haiti:

> ...Ti Noel comenzó a reconocer ciertos lugares... (123)
> ... Ti Noel descubría de pronto, con asombro, las pompas de un estilo napoleónico... (124)
> Al salir de una arboleda tuvo la impresión de penetrar en un suntuoso verjel. (125)
> A medida que se iba acercando, Ti Noel descubría terrazas, estatuas, arcadas... (126)
> ... vio que se trataba de una iglesia... (126)

These phrases indicate that, although the narrator views and describes Ti Noel, it is Ti Noel who views the scene. The reader is told only what is taken in by him. This distinction, as in the earlier examples referring to Pauline, allows the narrative to be tinged with the subjectivity of the characters. Thus, the world focalized by Pauline is coloured by her sensual personality, while Christophe's palace at Millot, when focalized by Ti Noel, is described in the terms of his astonishment at seeing it. In both cases, the perception of reality by the character confirms the stance adopted by the narrator. While Pauline's distorted image of herself and her environment reflects the artificiality of her culture, the discrepancy between Ti Noel's expectations and what he actually sees in Haiti reaffirms the difference in outlook between the New World Africans and the European and Europeanized characters. As a result of extensive focalization by characters in *El reino de este mundo* Ti Noel is frequently referred to by critics as the interpreter of the world described in the novel. This impression, however, is the inevitable consequence of the proportionally greater role given to him in comparison with other characters. In fact, the focalizers change according to the incidents narrated and the appropriateness of characters as a lens through which to view the world. Thus, in 'Ultima ratio regum', the focalizer is mainly Christophe, while in 'La noche de las estatuas' Solimán is an important source of focalization. In all cases, however, the narrator retains his position as the primary focalizer and uses the characters in a secondary role.

The control exerted by the narrator is equally evident in the forms of speech used in the novel. The text has very few examples of direct speech. The longest passage is the brief paragraph containing Bouckman's final admonition to the conspirators (79). The only passages of dialogue are three exchanges of two lines each in which Ti Noel asks the bookseller about the prints (26-7), asks where the dogs loaded in Santiago are being taken (101-2), and protests his conscription into Christophe's labour force. There are a few statements of a single line each: Mackandal's decision to escape from Lenormand's estate (41), the exclamation from the crowd at Mackandal's salvation from the fire (66), Governor Rochambeau's determination to use dogs against the rebels (115), Christophe's reaction to the drums that signal the impending rebellion against him (155), and the suggestion made by one of Christophe's former prisoners that Queen María Luisa suffer the same fate as her husband (166). For the rest, the voices of the characters are heard only in a number of interpolated texts: the Creole songs and invocations of the negroes (60, 62, 79, 80, 180), the recitation of extracts from Racine's *Phèdre*, two lines of a French song (95), and the liturgical texts in 'Crónica del 15 de agosto' (147-50). Indirect or reported speech is just as infrequent. It is used, for instance, to convey Lenormand's request for a grinding stone to sharpen a machete when preparing to amputate Mackandal's arm (36) and to report Ti Noel's misleading explanation of the death of Lenormand's prize cows (46).

The infrequency of these forms of speech underlines the unimportance of dialogue as a narrative technique but does not mean that the characters are entirely silent. They speak indirectly, through the narrator. Just as the narrator employs the characters as focalizers and makes their point of view part of his own description and narrative of events, he also assimilates their discourse to his own. On some occasions the narrator simply mentions the theme of the character's conversation. Thus, the general content of the stories told by the colonists during the search for Mackandal is described (54) without narrating the stories themselves. The tales about Mackandal and the songs taught by Ti Noel to his children are merely alluded to (76) without actually being given. With the exception of a short paragraph, referred to above, the text of Bouckman's speech to the conspirators is not reproduced. The substance of what he says is conveyed by the description of his voice and the effects of his words on Ti Noel (78). Only the essential points of Leclerc's conversation with his wife are given by the narrator (106), while the actual conversation is omitted. The tendency of the narrator to assume responsibility for the speech of the characters is, of course, best exemplified by the account of Pauline's visit to Haiti, which is introduced as if it were news received by Ti Noel from informants but is told entirely by the narrator.

Indirect free speech is related to the technique referred to above, but is used much more extensively.[9] It entails the free reproduction by the narrator of the words spoken by a character without acknowledging them as. such by placing them between quotation marks. In addition to allowing the narrator to report the characters' speech without allowing them to intervene directly, it permits him to distance himself from their opinions and to describe the different views of the world held by the characters

[9] For a fuller discussion of this form, see Brian McHale, 'Free Indirect Discourse: A Survey of Recent Accounts', *PTL: A Journal for Descriptive Poetics and Theory of Literature*, 3 (1978), 249-87.

themselves. The first chapter of the novel, for example, contains an extended passage contrasting African and European kings (27-9). The narrator makes it clear, however, that the categorical distinction between them is not his own. Thus, the final part of the passage is introduced by the phrase 'Ti Noel había sido instruido en esas verdades por el profundo saber de Mackandal' (28). Although the text that follows, beginning 'En el Africa, el rey era guerrero...', is not given in quotation marks, its source has been clearly identified as 'verdades ...de Mackandal'. The text is therefore accepted as a free transcription either of Mackandal's own speech or of Ti Noel's recollection of it. This procedure is also adopted in the first half of the following chapter, 'La poda'. After a description of Ti Noel's fascination by Mackandal and the attraction of the mandinga's voice, the free reproduction of Mackandal's words is signalled by the following sentence: 'El mozo comprendía, al oírlo, que el Cabo Francés, con sus campanarios, sus edificios de cantería, sus casas normandas guarnecidas de larguísimos balcones techados, era bien poca cosa en comparación con las ciudades de Guinea' (33-4). The remainder of the paragraph, beginning 'Allá había cúpulas de barro encarnado...' (34-5), therefore conveys a description that is clearly derived from Mackandal. By a similar use of this technique in a later chapter the narrator describes the metamorphoses of Mackandal in such a way that they appear as an objective reality when seen from the point of view of the negroes: 'Todos sabían que la iguana verde, la mariposa nocturna, el perro desconocido, el alcatraz inverosímil, no eran simples disfraces...' (55-6). The phrase 'Todos sabían' at the beginning of the sentence indicates, however, that the narrator is not really conveying objective facts, but the freely transcribed opinions of those who believe in Mackandal's metamorphoses. The use of indirect free speech is particularly important in describing the negroes' conviction that Mackandal will escape execution by using his power of lycanthropy:

Los amos interrogaron las caras de sus esclavos con la mirada. Pero los negros mostraban una despechante indiferencia. ¿Qué sabían los blancos de cosas de negros? En sus ciclos de metamorfosis, Mackandal se había adentrado muchas veces en el mundo arcano de los insectos, desquitándose de la falta de un brazo humano con la posesión de varias patas, de cuatro élitros o de largas antenas. Había sido mosca, ciempiés, falena, comején, tarántula, vaquita de San Antón y hasta cocuyo de grandes luces verdes. En el momento decisivo, las ataduras del mandinga, privadas de un cuerpo que atar, dibujarían por un segundo el contorno de un hombre de aire, antes de resbalar a lo largo del poste. Y Mackandal, transformado en mosquito zumbón, iría a posarse en el mismo tricornio del jefe de las tropas, para gozar del desconcierto de los blancos. (64-5)

Although reported objectively by the narrator as part of his own discourse, Mackandal's expected metamorphosis and escape are 'cosas de negros', firmly believed in by them but not shared by others. The proof of this occurs later in the same chapter when the two versions of Mackandal's execution are reported (65-7).

Indirect free speech is also used to transmit the view of the world held by the European characters. In 'La llamada de los caracoles' Lenormand's anxiety at the state of affairs in the colony is communicated by a free reproduction of Governor Blanchelande's opinions on the effects of the spread of liberalism (83-4). Similarly, after the slave rebellion, in 'Dogón dentro del arca', the technique is used to convey the reaction of both Blanchelande and Lenormand to the chaos of Saint-Domingue (89-91). Whenever indirect free speech is employed, a signal is given to the reader that indicates a change of view and the free transcription of the words of a character. Thus, Blanchelande's opinion of the chaos after the rebellion is conveyed in the passage beginning 'La anarquía se entronizaba en el mundo...' (90), but the reader has been prepared by the previous sentence to expect a change in focus and the shift to some form of reproduction of the Governor's speech: 'Difícil era sacar una orientación precisa de su desordenado monólogo, en que los vituperios a los filósofos alternaban con citas de agoreros fragmentos de cartas suyas, enviadas a París, y que no habían sido contestadas siquiera' (89-90). What the reader receives, then, is the narrator's free version of Blanchelande's monologue as heard by Lenormand.

The effect of indirect forms of speech is similar to that obtained by using the characters as focalizers. Both techniques permit the narrator to filter a major part of the narrative through the characters. Thus, although the narrator retains control, the text frequently incorporates two levels of interpretation. On one level, the narrator maintains a global view of events and is accepted as a reliable witness by the reader, if only because the text provides no reason to doubt him. At the same time, the narrator's global perspective encompasses the characters' more limited views, the sources of which are constantly identified through the techniques of narration employed. There is, however, a fundamental difference between the narrator and the characters. Whereas the former may be capable of giving an objective view of events, the latter are entirely subjective and their opinions are much less reliable because they are consistently discredited by a narrator who does not accept them as his own. This distinction provides an important basis for evaluating the content of the novel and establishing how certain aspects of 'lo real maravilloso' are incorporated into the text. Carpentier writes in the prologue that the marvellous presupposes a faith (11) and that the miracle of Mackandal's salvation from his executioners is a product of the faith of his followers (13). However, neither the reader nor the narrator of *El reino de este mundo* has the same faith. Consequently, although Mackandal's metamorphoses are real enough to those who believe in them, they cannot be described objectively without violating our sense of what is empirically possible. The problem is overcome by focalization and indirect free speech, which permit the narrator to give an apparently objective description of what is really a subjective view held by those whose beliefs differ from ours. Although the techniques of narration, the two versions of Mackandal's execution, and the reader's own incredulity are sufficient to discredit the veracity of Mackandal's metamorphoses and salvation, the actual convictions of his followers are not challenged, but affirmed. Thus the form of narration in *El reino de este mundo* assists in underlining Carpentier's idea of the marvellous. The marvellous is not the product of empirical reality and is not described as such in the novel. It is the result of changes in perception engendered by what is believed to be real. Whether or not Carpentier actually succeeds in communicating a sensation of the marvellous to the reader by this method is a different matter and has been discussed in an earlier chapter. Yet, regardless of whether or not he is able to inscribe the marvellous in his text, the interplay between objective reality and subjective belief, like that between the narrator and the characters, pervades the entire text. Since much of *El reino de este mundo* is based on narrative techniques that imply the indirect description of views held by the characters, the novel may be considered as a work that focuses on how reality is perceived. Given that all perceptions are subjective, they are to some extent equal, but the stance adopted by the narrator, who must be accepted as the only reliable interpreter of the world described in the novel, inclines the reader to give a more positive reception to the dynamic view of the negro than to the decadent view of the European. The narrator therefore tells the story in such a way that he confirms the message which, as we have seen, is also implied by the structure of its content.

Intertextuality

Although I have discussed the historical sources of *El reino de este mundo* and the aesthetic principles of Carpentier in earlier chapters, it must be acknowledged that works of literature are generally read without benefit of a detailed knowledge of their sources, the identity and intentions of the author, the influences on his work, or the circumstances of composition. Lack of this information perhaps limits our understanding of the total work, but is not an absolute barrier to an intelligent reading. The plot and the structure of a narrative, the symbolic dimension of incidents and characters, and the role of an implied or dramatized narrator are among the resources exploited by the novelist in creating an autonomous world. Nevertheless, demands are often made on the reader which implicitly require him to resort to a knowledge not acquired from the text. An author may presup-

pose the reader's ability to perceive the relation between the text
and its sources. More commonly, he makes allusions that occasionally oblige it to be read in the light of particular phenomena,
such as a painting, a character or a passage from a work of fiction, a musical composition, or an historical incident. Such
phenomena acquire the status of secondary texts and, by the
mere fact that they are alluded to, implicitly contribute to the
text in which they are mentioned. Carpentier appears to fall
readily into this category of authors. One of the characteristics
of his narrative technique is the frequent allusion to a variety of
cultural and historical phenomena that lead the reader to complete the text by appealing to his own knowledge. It is this practice and its implications in *El reino de este mundo* that I propose
to examine under the heading of intertextuality.

The history of Haiti and the various historical works used by
Carpentier when writing *El reino de este mundo* underlie virtually the entire novel. Yet the plot is independent of its sources. As
my analysis has shown, history is interpreted anew. The changes
in chronology, the selective use of historical incidents, and the
organization of the narrative in favour of a cyclical rather than a
linear view of events indicate a departure from an interpretation
offered by a conventional work of history. Although the sources
might be thought of as a kind of text of which the novel is but a
parallel version, they do not constitute a co-text in conjunction
with which the novel must be read in order for it to be
understood. In much the same way as our knowledge of reality
permits us to evaluate any work of fiction, the general historical
sources of *El reino de este mundo* have the tacit role of authenticating the text. Thus, the knowledgeable reader endorses many
passages of description and the narration of incidents such as
Bouckman's conspiracy or the last days of Christophe because
he recognizes their factual bases. The less informed reader
evidently loses something, but his loss is compensated by his
ability to evaluate the novel much as he would judge any purely
fictional work which is accepted or rejected in the light of its internal coherence and appropriateness as a simulation of the real
world.

The general history of Haiti and many of its details do not

promote intertextual relations whereby the reader is constantly obliged to complete the text by making the appropriate connection with its sources. The narrative style of *El reino de este mundo* is certainly laconic, but the narrative omits none of the information essential for its continuity and understanding. The lapses in time between each part are bridged without the reader's having to fill the gaps from his own knowledge. Narrative continuity is maintained and historical change is described exclusively in terms of what the reader has already learned from the novel. As we have seen, the first chapter of Part I serves as an introduction by providing the context within which the plot is developed. In the first chapter of Part II, 'La hija de Minos y de Pasifae', the growth of Saint-Domingue is described and related to changes in Lenormand's household. The information may be easily assimilated against the background of what has been learned from Part I. At the beginning of 'Los signos', the first chapter of Part III, it is clear that Ti Noel returns to Haiti after a prolonged absence. Before embarking on a description of Christophe's regime, which is a new element in the novel, an appropriate context is created and the continuity of the narrative is established by a brief account of Lenormand's death and the circumstances in which Ti Noel obtained his freedom. Moreover, although the description of Christophe's palace implies a new development, its introduction relies on a familiarity with Ti Noel, whose gradual realization of the implications of what he discovers parallels that of the reader. A similar procedure is adopted at the beginning of Part IV. The first two chapters, 'La noche de las estatuas' and 'La real casa', bring the reader up to date immediately by focusing on what has happened to characters who are already known to us from earlier parts of the text. Thus, the former chapter deals with the life in Italy of the survivors of Christophe's household, while the latter relates what has become of Ti Noel since the death of the King. The new situation in Haiti, the appearance of the 'Mulatos Republicanos', is introduced abruptly, but is presented as an event that disturbs the life of Ti Noel, with which we have again become familiar.

The economy of the narrative and the reduction of the role of history as necessary for its understanding are particularly evident in the techniques used to introduce major characters and incidents. The account of Bouckman's conspiracy in 'El Pacto Mayor' is not an immediate continuation of events from the chapter before it, which contains a description of the changes in Saint-Domingue and Lenormand's household during the years after the execution of Mackandal. In the light of the enmity between the colonists and their slaves, a further rebellion by the latter may well be expected, but no account of the precise circumstances that preceded the conspiracy is given. Nevertheless the reader is not expected to supply them from his own knowledge, since the text establishes its own continuity. The chapter before 'El Pacto Mayor', ending with a brief paragraph describing how Ti Noel instructs his children in their African heritage, concludes with this sentence: 'Además, bueno era recordar a menudo al Manco, puesto que el Manco, alejado de estas tierras por tareas de importancia, regresaría a ellas el día menos pensado' (76). The continuation of the text is the first sentence of 'El Pacto Mayor': 'Los truenos parecían romperse en aludes sobre los riscosos perfiles del Morne Rouge' (77). This is not the first time, however, that the reappearance of Mackandal is mentioned and alluded to in conjunction with the violence of nature. The two sentences quoted above combine the same ideas expressed on an earlier occasion, before Mackandal's capture, when his return and its consequences are also foreshadowed: 'Un día daría la señal del gran levantamiento, y los Señores de Allá, encabezados por Damballah, por el Amo de los Caminos y por Ogún de los Hierros, traerían el rayo y el trueno, para desencadenar el ciclón que completaría la obra de los hombres' (56). Although not directly announced, Bouckman's conspiracy is nonetheless foreshadowed by the text. As a prelude to the 'gran levantamiento' expected by Mackandal's followers, it is also foretold by Ti Noel's admonition to his children to remember Mackandal and await his return. Of course, Mackandal does not reappear, but the rebellion recalls his spirit, and Bouckman's personality and commanding voice (78) are reminiscent of qualities attributed to the earlier rebel leader (33).

A similar use of textual association is used to introduce

Christophe in Part III. His name is not mentioned in Part III until after the description of his palace, giving the reader ample opportunity to assimilate the new environment encountered by Ti Noel. Then, when Christophe's name is mentioned, it is placed in a context with which the reader has already been made familiar: 'Ti Noel comprendió que se hallaba en Sans-Souci, la residencia del rey Henri Christophe, aquel que fuera antaño cocinero en la calle de los Españoles, dueño del albergue de *La Corona*...' (127-8). As I have already mentioned, Christophe's ownership of La Corona is referred to twice in Part II. How he rose from pastrycook to king is of no importance for the novel. The earlier references to him, however slight, are sufficient for the reader to locate him in the text when he is introduced in Part III and to create a sense of continuity without the need to look for further explanations in sources. In contrast to the reintroduction of Christophe, the appearance of Pauline Bonaparte seems to disrupt the continuity of the narrative and is foreshadowed only by the brief reference that precedes it (102) to the arrival of news in Santiago de Cuba from Cap Français. In some respects the disruption is appropriate. Pauline's visit and her view of colonial life from the perspective of Europe are by nature intrusive. Even so, few concessions are made to the historically uninformed reader and little information is given concerning her background. Although her behaviour and attitudes establish her as a person of some social prominence and doubtful morality, her identity is not immediately clarified. She is referred to as the wife of General Leclerc soon after she is introduced (103), but is not identified as a Bonaparte (105) until after her character is clearly described. Thus, just as the historical events of the French invasion are subordinated to a description of Pauline's experiences in Saint-Domingue, her importance as an historical figure is diminished. Interest centres on her principally because of the nature of her character. By the same token, when she is referred to later in the novel, in 'La noche de las estatuas', allusions to her life during the intervening years are omitted entirely and the reader is not told of the circumstances that made it possible for Solimán to find a statue of her in the Borghese Palace. The knowledgeable reader, of course, is aware that she married into the Borghese family. However, as in the case of Bouckman's conspiracy and Christophe's rise from pastrycook to king, the narrative, not history, provides the source of continuity. The later references to Pauline are in fact anticipated in the text in the description of her departure from Saint-Domingue: 'En la cesta que contenía sus ajados disfraces de criolla viajaba un amuleto a Papá Legba, trabajado por Solimán, destinado a abrir a Pauline Bonaparte todos los caminos que la condujeron a Roma' (114).

In the light of the preceding comments, we may attribute a double function to the foreshadowing of characters and incidents. It is part of the cyclical structure of the text, as shown in the previous chapter, and is also one of the devices that allows this structure to exist independently of its sources. Yet, regardless of the use of techniques to reduce the role of history as a necessary adjunct of the text, there are still numerous occasions on which the reader is called upon to complete the meaning by establishing intertextual relations with phenomena external to the novel.

The titles of Carpentier's novels often have evident associations or give an ironic meaning to an established phrase. *El siglo de las luces* (1962) is an ironic use of a phrase conventionally employed to describe the eighteenth century, in which most of the novel is set. *El recurso del método* (1974) is a parody of the title of Descartes' *Discourse on Method*. *La consagración de la primavera* (1978) is an allusion to the well-known musical composition by Igor Stravinsky, *The Rite of Spring*. The title of *El reino de este mundo* occurs twice in the novel (66 and 197) and acquires an appropriate meaning when viewed solely in the light of these contexts. But it also has Biblical connotations: 'And the seventh angel sounded the trumpet: and there were great voices in heaven, saying: The kingdom of this world is become our Lord's and his Christ's, and he shall reign for ever and ever' (Revelation, xi.15). The association between the novel and this passage, however, is ironic.

The text provides several reasons for identifying Ti Noel with Christ. By expecting Mackandal's return and its consequences, Ti Noel preaches a Second Coming that entails a settlement of accounts akin to the Biblical Armageddon. His name associates him with the Nativity and, therefore, with Christ, while the instruction he gives his twelve children (74 and 76) recalls the relation between Jesus and the twelve disciples. Towards the end of the novel, Ti Noel also appears to be preparing to sacrifice himself. He, too, has his Palm Sunday: 'Cuando las mujeres lo veían aparecer en un sendero, agitaban paños claros, en señal de reverencia, como las palmas que un domingo habían festejado a Jesús' (183). Moreover, just as Christ, after his final entry into Jerusalem, spoke at length to his disciples of the Second Coming and the destruction of the city (Matthew xxiv, Mark xiii, Luke xxi), Ti Noel also addresses his people as a prophet: 'Llevado a un toque de tambores, Ti Noel había caído en posesión del rey de Angola, pronunciando un largo discurso lleno de adivinanzas y de promesas' (183-4). The title of the final chapter, 'Agnus Dei' (Lamb of God), is the term traditionally used to identify Christ as a sacrificial victim, but is used here in reference to Ti Noel, who sacrifices himself to lead his people against their new masters. Finally, the apocalyptic ending to the novel implies the fulfilment of the prophecies alluded to earlier in that the reference to 'el derrumbe de las últimas ruinas de la antigua hacienda' (198) recalls the prophecy of Christ concerning the temple of Jerusalem that 'there shall not be left a stone upon a stone that shall not be thrown down' (Luke xxi.6; cf. Matthew xxiv.2, Mark xiii.2). In spite of these similarities and associations, however, there is an important difference. The teaching of Christ and the verse of Revelation from which the title of the novel is taken refer to the passing of the Kingdom of this World in favour of the Kingdom of Heaven. But, when Ti Noel understands that Mackandal's final metamorphosis was intended to allow him to remain among men (66), the meaning of existence becomes clearer and he reaches the conclusion that Man's destiny is on earth among his own kind:

> En el Reino de los Cielos no hay grandeza que conquistar, puesto que allá todo es jerarquía establecida, incógnita despejada, existir sin término, imposibilidad de sacrificio, reposo y deleite. Por ello, agobiado de penas y de Tareas,

> hermoso dentro de su miseria, capaz de amar en medio de
> las plagas, el hombre sólo puede hallar su grandeza, su
> máxima medida en el Reino de este Mundo. (197)

Ti Noel is a Christ figure, portrayed in the novel as a follower of
Mackandal and an eventual teacher, leader, and prophet, but his
life does not embody the Christian message, a distinction which
reaffirms the fundamental conflict of the novel. Voodoo and
Christianity oppose each other, not only because they represent
the cultures of two antagonistic peoples at the beginning and the
end, respectively, of their development, but because they em-
brace different philosophies. The future glimpsed by Ti Noel for
which he sacrifices himself is not spiritual liberation in an
afterlife, but a continuing struggle on earth by successive generations for a freedom and happiness they will never fully obtain.
The title of *El reino de este mundo*, with its ironic evocation of a
familiar meaning, is therefore an appropriate means of succinctly summarizing one of the central issues of the novel.

Not surprisingly, the chapter headings have a comparable
function. Like the title of the novel, they are captions that effectively summarize important themes. The first three, 'Las cabezas
de cera', 'La poda', and 'Lo que hallaba la mano', for example,
are clearly used for this purpose. As we have mentioned
previously, a number of the headings also recall familiar ideas
which are given new associations when read in the context of the
novel. This is the case with 'De Profundis', 'Las metamorfosis',
'Sans-Souci', and 'Agnus Dei'. Alternatively, the opposition
between the familiar and the less familiar is occasionally a part
of the title itself, as in 'Dogón dentro del arca'. In all these cases,
the reader is evidently called upon to evoke the appropriate text
or association in order to complete the meaning.

The intertextual relation between *El reino de este mundo* and
other writings is more obvious when the latter are directly
quoted in the novel. Epigraphs are common in Carpentier's fiction. In *El siglo de las luces*, for example, he uses the captions
from Goya's *Los desastres de la guerra* (1863), and in *El recurso
del método* quotes from the writings of Descartes. The five
epigraphs in *El reino de este mundo* are from five different

sources. The first, from Cervantes's *Los trabajos de Persiles y Sigismunda* (1617), is placed before the prologue and referred to in the prologue itself (11), but it also serves the entire novel. This does not mean, however, that *El reino de este mundo* should be interpreted in the light of Cervantes's romance. Other than drawing attention to a belief in lycanthropy as one of the major themes, the epigraph tends to legitimize the theme itself both historically and artistically because it is referred to by no less an authority than Cervantes. The epigraphs to Parts I and IV are also taken from Spanish classical authors. The former is from a *comedia* by Lope de Vega, *El nuevo mundo descubierto por Colón* (probably written between 1598 and 1603), the latter from a piece by Calderón that I have not been able to identify. Reference to works by two of Spain's Golden Age dramatists is in keeping with Carpentier's writing as a whole. He frequently alludes to theatre and often uses the implications of role-playing as a means of character description. Moreover, his inclination for allegory has often led critics to remark on the association of aspects of his work with the Spanish *auto sacramental*, as, for example, in *El camino de Santiago* (first published in *Guerra del tiempo*, 1958, which also has an epigraph taken from Lope). There is no evidence that this relation is important to *El reino de este mundo*. The novel contains several allusions to theatre, which I have already mentioned, and the universal implications of Ti Noel's life make him a kind of Everyman, but the connection is not fully developed. Like the epigraph before the prologue, those taken from Lope de Vega and Calderón anticipate aspects of the novel. Thus, the quotation from Calderón at the beginning of Part IV anticipates Ti Noel's experience of the natural world through lycanthropy and its similarity with the world of men. The passage from Lope de Vega, however, has broader implications. Identification of the devil as 'El rey de Occidente' and his claim to possession of the New World even before the arrival of Columbus recall the European attitude to indigenous religions and the belief that they amounted to devil-worship. The appropriateness of the epigraph, therefore, is its relation to the confrontation in the New World between the Christian and the non-Christian cultures described in the novel.

It not only identifies the ideological bases of the conflict, but establishes the historical context of its origin. Nevertheless, in view of the negative description of the colonists in *El reino de este mundo*, Lope's text, like others alluded to in the novel, is to be understood ironically.

The two remaining epigraphs are not from literary sources. That to Part II is from the *Mémoires* of the Duchesse d'Abrantès (see note 3, above), while that to Part III is taken from an account of a visit to Haiti by the German geographer Karl Ritter (1779-1859).[10] With the exception of Carpentier's comments in the prologue, these two epigraphs are the most direct reminders of the relation between the novel and history. The passage by the Duchesse d'Abrantès establishes that Pauline's idealized version of the life that awaits her in the West Indies is not fictional. It has historical origins and is shared by others who view Haiti from the distance of Paris. The point is directly confirmed by the intertextuality of the epigraph and the narrative created by the reference to the Duchesse d'Abrantès as Pauline's advisor in matters of fashion (103). Karl Ritter's reference to the opulence of Christophe's court is also a reminder of the historical truth underlying the narrative, and the description of Ritter himself as a 'testigo del saqueo de Sans-Souci' (117) is an invitation to accept its veracity. The implication of both epigraphs, however indirect, is that significant elements of Parts II and III are to be accepted as authentic on the grounds that they are derived from the texts of historical witnesses.

In addition to the epigraphs, there are several other direct quotations. The passages in Creole are all attributed to negro characters. They include a song of celebration (60), a lament against slavery (62), and invocations to the Voodoo gods (79-80, 180). While contributing a measure of authenticity to the text, they are also a very concise way of completing the characterization of the black population of Haiti and its culture. The Latin texts must first be seen as a contrast to the passages in Creole. Unlike the latter, they belong to an adopted culture. Significant-

---

[10] *Naturhistorische Reise nach der westindischen Insel Hayti* (Stuttgart: Hallberger, 1938), p.78.

ly enough, Queen María Luisa does not fully understand them (147) and King Henri Christophe is unable to give them his complete attention because he is preoccupied by the probable conspiracy against him implied by the Voodoo practices of his subjects (148). The contrast among the Latin texts themselves emphasizes the underlying tension. As if in confirmation of Christophe's fears, the joyous lines from the liturgy of the Mass of the Assumption are replaced by the more ominous passages from the Mass for the Dead which are heard when Breille's ghost disrupts the ceremony. The extracts from Racine's *Phèdre* included earlier in the novel (75-6) also confirm the contrast between cultures. As I have already suggested, the slaves' reaction to Mlle Floridor's recitation confirms that the verses in French are to be taken ironically. Divorced from their original context, they acquire a literal meaning which demonstrates the cultural differences between Mlle Floridor and her listeners.

The range of possible meanings contributed by the quotation of texts by other authors depends, of course, on the ability of the reader to establish the appropriate connections. Their inclusion, however, establishes a specific link between the novel and the real world. Although *El reino de este mundo* may be thought of as describing a world that exists only by virtue of its creation in the text, the status of this world is affected by its association with other texts known to the reader. If Mlle Floridor can recite a text by Racine, if the Haitian royal family can listen to an authentic Roman liturgy, or if parts of the novel are endorsed by a known German geographer, then the content of the novel is more credible and the characters can be accepted more readily as if they were real. Thus, in addition to contributing a possible range of meanings to the novel, one of the prime functions of the intertextual relation between *El reino de este mundo* and other writings, whether their origin is literary, historical, liturgical or folkloric, is to appeal to the reader's sense of reality. In this respect, their purpose is akin to that of some of the allusions to history that are an important part of the text.

Although references to historical persons, places, and events encountered on almost every page of *El reino de este mundo* are not all of the same quality, they frequently demand the same

response. Many are bounded by the context in which they occur
and are directly accepted as part of the world described in the
novel without the reader's searching for confirmation of their
existence in the real world. This is the case of the persons referred to as Mackandal's collaborators:

> en la añilería del Dondón podía contar con Olaín el
> hortelano, con Romaine, la cocinera de los barracones,
> con el tuerto Jean-Pierrot; en cuanto a la hacienda de
> Lenormand de Mezy, había enviado mensajes a los tres
> hermanos Pongué, a los congos nuevos, al fula patizambo
> y a Marinette, la mulata que había dormido, en otros tiem-
> pos, en la cama del amo... (45)

Apart from the reference to Lenormand, there is no hint that
these persons are historical, and it would take a certain effort to
verify a point which would not necessarily add anything to the
meaning of the text. Yet persons whose historical identity may
be corroborated more easily or whose names are already familiar
to the reader are mentioned in exactly the same manner. During
the hunt for Mackandal, for instance, the colonists idle away
their time telling tales of their ancestors:

> ...se evocaban las hazañas de abuelos que habían tomado
> parte en el saqueo de Cartagena de Indias o habían hun-
> dido las manos en el tesoro de la corona española cuando
> Piet Hein, pata de palo, lograra en aguas cubanas la
> fabulosa hazaña soñada por los corsarios durante cerca de
> dos siglos. Sobre mesas manchadas de vinazo, en el ir y
> venir de los tiros de dados, se proponían brindis a
> l'Esnambuc, a Bertrand d'Ogeron, a Du Rausset y a los
> hombres de pelo en pecho que habían creado la colonia por
> su cuenta y riesgo... (54)

The difference between the two passages is that the latter expects
a certain response. The reader is expected to remember part of
the history of the Caribbean and to recall the names and deeds
of well-known buccaneers. As a result, he is then able to

acknowledge the historical authenticity of the colonists by virtue of the fact that they are the descendants of famous historical figures. As part of the text, however, both Mackandal's collaborators and the colonists' ancestors belong equally to the world described by the novel. Both are therefore to be accepted on the same terms. By accepting one group as authentic, the other, by implication, must be given the same measure of credibility.

The use of the technique referred to above means that the reader has only to recognize part of the novel as belonging to his own world in order to integrate the remainder to it. For this reason, the text need contain no explicit statements concerning its historical validity. In many instances they would be clearly redundant. The references to the Declaration of the Rights of Man (81), to the Café de la Régence, to Jean-Jacques Rousseau as 'el vicario saboyano' (83-4), and to the French Romantics who influenced Pauline's view of reality (106-7) require no explanation. As in the case of the pirates who founded Saint-Domingue, the reader tacitly provides the necessary corroboration and commentary from his own knowledge. Indeed, the text relies on this kind of reader participation. Knowing about the pirates of the Caribbean, the pride that the colonists have in them as their ancestors tells us what the colonists themselves must be like and how little they respect authority. Similarly, our familiarity with the French Romantics and the susceptibility of people such as Pauline to the influence of their work avoids the need for a lengthy description. In other instances, when less familiar matters of history or lesser-known persons are referred to, the text is a little more explicit. Thus the identity of Moreau de Saint Mery and Alexander Exquemelin and their connection with the Caribbean are briefly explained:

Ahora [Lenormand] recordaba que, años atrás, aquel rubicundo y voluptuoso abogado del Cabo que era Moreau de Saint Mery había recogido algunos datos sobre las prácticas salvajes de los hechiceros de las montañas, apuntando que algunos negros eran ofidiólatras. (90-1)
Los primeros días [Pauline] se distrajo bañándose en una

ensenada arenosa y hojeando las memorias del cirujano
Alejandro Oliverio Oexmelin, que tan bien había conocido
los hábitos y fechorías de los corsarios y bucaneros de
América... (109)

The identification of the authors of the epigraphs appears to
follow a similar criterion. Cervantes, Lope de Vega, and
Calderón need no introduction. The Duchesse d'Abrantès and
Karl Ritter are not so well known, however. By identifying them
briefly, the former as a friend of Pauline Bonaparte, the latter as
a witness of the last days of Christophe, the intertextual relations are established more firmly and the reader is able to locate
both persons in an appropriate context.

Style
The interplay between the known and the unknown is also an
important factor in the style of *El reino de este mundo*. In
'Problemática de la actual novela latinoamericana' (see note 1,
above) Carpentier devotes a section to style and ends with the
statement, 'El legítimo estilo del novelista latinoamericano actual es el barroco' (43). His conclusion is partly related to his
opinion concerning art in Latin America: 'Nuestro arte siempre
fue barroco: desde la espléndida escultura precolombina y el de
los códices, hasta la mejor novelística actual de América, pasán-
dose por las catedrales y monasterios coloniales de nuestro con-
tinente' (42-3). But it is principally derived from his belief that
the baroque style is particularly suited to the novelist's task of
describing an unknown continent in terms that will make it
familiar and allow it to be perceived as a palpable reality. As an
example of what he means he refers to Albrecht Dürer's well-
known drawing of a rhinoceros:

Obsérvese cuán barroco resulta, en la obra de Durero,
maestro de la parquedad, la estampa del Rinoceronte. Es
porque el Rinoceronte era, en su época, un animal nuevo,
forastero, salido de lo desconocido, perteneciente a una
heráldica de selvas ignotas, de paisajes inimaginables. Por
lo tanto, había que detallarlo, que mostrarlo, con todas sus

armaduras y costras, aún emparentado, vagamente, con el
Dragón la Tarasca, de las mascaradas medioevales. (41)

Statements such as these, frequently endorsed in lectures and in-
terviews given by Carpentier, have firmly established the idea
that the baroque quality of his prose is one of its outstanding
characteristics. Nevertheless, a systematic study of his style,
based on the meaning of the term baroque and Carpentier's conception of it, has yet to be made. Among essays devoted to *El
reino de este mundo*, Jorge Dávila Vázquez's application of
criteria proposed by Helmut Hatzfeld (*15*) points in one of the
directions that might be taken profitably. Since my comments
on style in *El reino de este mundo* can only touch on what is
evidently a major undertaking, I shall limit myself to a brief
assessment of how the techniques of description emphasize the
visual qualities of the novel with the purpose of making the
unknown more easily recognizable.

In some respects, the meticulous detail referred to by
Carpentier in his essay is more characteristic of his later novels
than of *El reino de este mundo*, which contains no lengthy
descriptions comparable to those of the jungle in *Los pasos perdidos* (1953) or the sea in *El siglo de las luces*. Although the
description of the plants and their properties discovered by
Mackandal (37-8) or the changes in marine life noted by Pauline
Bonaparte as she sails beyond the Azores (104) anticipate a later
development in Carpentier's style, detailed description of the
natural world is not a characteristic of *El reino de este mundo*.
Moreover, he does not dwell on single objects, however unfamiliar they might be, with the purpose of describing them as
fully as possible. Details are important in *El reino de este mundo*, but rather than minutely drawn miniatures, they contribute
large images intended to convey a particular historical context, a
certain atmosphere, or a particular event. This effect is often
achieved metonymically by alluding to an object or action which
is often no more than a mere detail but is sufficient to convey an
entire scene.

In some instances a particular context is described by considering it from several points of reference. The success of the

first chapter in establishing the social and historical context of the novel depends on the associations among the different heads seen or remembered by Ti Noel. None of them is described in great detail, but the mere mention of their salient features is sufficient for the reader to visualize them and to grasp more easily how they are interpreted by Ti Noel. A comparable procedure is used at the beginning of 'La llamada de los caracoles' where eighteenth-century French liberalism is described through a series of direct and indirect references to a philosopher, an artist, a poet, a novelist, politicians, and a traveller of the period who embody a concept of colonial life that Lenormand and his fellow colonists consider as idealized. Although each reference is no more than a detail, sometimes little more than a name, the accumulation of them all and their associations for the reader amount to a complex image of the situation which the colonists believe is threatening them. In other chapters a complete scene is presented through the combination of a number of brief allusions. The interior of the Cathedral in Santiago de Cuba, for example, is described with a series of details that give a vivid impression of the entire place:

> Los oros del barroco, las cabelleras humanas de los Cristos, el misterio de los confesionarios recargados de molduras, el can de los dominicos, los dragones aplastados por santos pies, el cerdo de San Antón, el color quebrado de San Benito, las Vírgenes negras, los San Jorge con coturnos y juboncillos de actores de tragedia francesa, los instrumentos pastoriles tañidos en noches de pascuas... (98)

The description of Sans-Souci (125-9) follows the same pattern. Although it is not described systematically, a complete impression of the place is conveyed by referring to the activities of people seen by Ti Noel. In fact the paragraph expressing Ti Noel's surprise on realizing that everyone is black (127) amounts to a descriptive list. In other places a vivid impression of events is obtained from a few details of relatively minor importance. The attack against the colonists during the slave rebellion, for example, is represented by a few striking images of incidents on Lenormand's estate, including the pillaging of his cellar:

> Riendo y peleando, los negros resbalaban sobre un jaboncillo de orégano, tomates adobados, alcaparras y huevas de arenque, que clareaba, sobre el suelo de ladrillo, el chorrear de un odrecillo de aceite rancio. Un negro desnudo se había metido, por broma, dentro de un tinajón lleno de manteca de cerdo. Dos viejas peleaban, en congo, por una olla de barro. (86)

In addition to the same pictorial quality, the account of the flight of Christophe's courtiers from Sans-Souci later in the novel has similar touches of humour, as in the following two passages, which convey the scene as effectively as a lengthy description:

> De pronto, Christophe observó que los músicos de la capilla real atravesaban el patio de honor, cargando con sus instrumentos. Cada cual se acompañaba de su deformación profesional. El arpista estaba encorvado, como giboso, por el peso del arpa; aquel otro, tan flaco, estaba como grávido de una tambora colgada de los hombros; otro se abrazaba a un helicón. Y cerraba la marcha un enano, caso oculto por el pabellón de un chinesco, que a cada paso tintineaba por todas las campanillas. (154)
> Un soldado palúdico, sorprendido por el motín, salió de la enfermería envuelto en una sábana, ajustándose el barbuquejo de un chacó. Al pasar debajo de la ventana de Christophe hizo un gesto obsceno y escapó a todo correr. (155)

The techniques referred to above stress the visual impact of the text, giving it the quality of a series of crowded baroque canvasses. From the beginning of the novel, through the images of the heads, and, in particular, through the prints contemplated by Ti Noel, the reader becomes accustomed to the pictorial quality of the text and a tendency to develop the narrative in

terms of a series of visual images. On a few occasions, such as in
the first chapter, in the comparison between the print hanging
on the wall and the position of Mlle Floridor's body after her
death, or in the references to the mirrors in Sans-Souci (156,
161), this tendency is promoted by the text itself. As a major
characteristic of Carpentier's style, it is also fostered by other
characteristics. The virtual absence of dialogue and the lack of
extended passages of commentary place greater emphasis on the
narration of events and description. At the same time, the
fragmentation of the narrative, both into four parts and into
chapters, enhances the impression that *El reino de este mundo* is
composed of a succession of vivid images.

Having referred already to the relative autonomy of each of
the four parts, I need not dwell further on their quality as extended images of different stages in the history of Haiti. It is
worthy of note, however, that each chapter, centred on one action or theme, also has a degree of autonomy. The conspiracy
described in 'El Pacto Mayor' has a number of visual elements,
including the dark, stormy night, Bouckman's harangue to the
assembled slaves, the Voodoo ceremony and the sacrifice of a
pig, that easily allow the scene to be pictured as a single image.
'Santiago de Cuba' is a busier, brighter canvas, but centres on
the life of the exiled colonists whose reactions to their loss of
land and status are briefly enumerated. 'El sacrificio de los
toros' centres on the construction of Christophe's citadel, conveying a picture which symbolizes the vanity of human pride and
has reminded critics of the building of the Tower of Babel in
paintings such as that by the elder Brueghel. The relative
autonomy of the chapters is also enhanced by their brevity and
by the development of the narrative so that it appears to progress as a series of scenes. Part II, for instance, has the following
sequence: Cap Français and Lenormand's household some years
after the execution of Mackandal ('La hija de Minos y de
Pasifae'); Bouckman's conspiracy on the Bois Caimán ('El
Pacto Mayor'); Lenormand's worries and the outbreak of the
rebellion ('La llamada de los caracoles'); the immediate after-
math of the rebellion ('Dogón dentro del arca'); the life of the
exiles ('Santiago de Cuba'); Pauline's idyllic life in Saint-

Domingue ('La nave de los perros'); and the chaos of disease and war ('San Trastorno'). Although the continuity of events persists, when described in these terms the chapters have the quality of a sequence of semi-independent scenes in which the title to each is a caption comparable to that given to a drawing or painting.

As part of a descriptive style intended to show an unfamiliar reality to the reader, the brief vivid scenes of *El reino de este mundo* should also be associated with Carpentier's assertion in 'Problemática de la actual novela latinoamericana' that the novelist should name the reality he describes: '...resulta que ahora nosotros, novelistas latinoamericanos, tenemos que nombrarlo todo —todo lo que nos define, envuelve y circunda: todo lo que opera con energía de *contexto*— para situarlo en lo universal' (42). The novelist should not apologize for his language and should abandon some of the practices of earlier fiction: 'Termináronse los tiempos de las novelas con glosarios adicionales para explicar lo que son *curiaras*, *polleras*, *arepas* o *cachazas*. Termináronse los tiempos de las novelas con llamadas al pie de la página para explicarnos que el árbol llamado de tal modo se viste de flores encarnadas en el mes de mayo o de agosto' (42).

The practice of naming things in *El reino de este mundo* is reflected in its vocabulary and use of proper nouns. The accumulation of proper nouns in the text is partly the consequence of meticulous use of historical sources. Carpentier constantly refers to the names of people and things regardless of whether or not they are important for the narrative: the man-of-war that sails into Cap Français (*La Courageuse*, 30); the ships on which Pauline sails (*El Océano*, 102; the *Switshure* [sic], 113); the newspapers available to the colonists (24, 71); Mackandal's collaborators (45); the Chief of Police who accompanies the French invasion of Saint-Domingue (105); and the five pageboys who served in Christophe's court (157). Since the naming of things gives identity and substance to all that belongs to the world described in the novel, the practice enhances the sense of reality attributed to it by the reader. In the case of unfamiliar proper nouns, our understanding is not seriously inhibited because they

acquire an autonomous meaning within the text. But the un-
familiarity of much of Carpentier's vocabulary frequently
makes considerable demands of the reader. The following
words, for example, are taken from the first few chapters:
garañones, *percherona*, *rocallas*, *guadralpas*, *rigodón*,
chifonías, *espolón*, *cuarterona*, *bululú*, *pífanos*, *mandinga*,
bucanes, *cimarrón*, *calendas*, *perinés*, *líticos*, *almirez*. They include americanisms, archaisms, erudite forms, neologisms, or
simply words that are not commonly used. The difficulty of
Carpentier's vocabulary is often a consequence of the need to
use unfamiliar language when naming unfamiliar objects, a
situation compounded by the fact that *El reino de este mundo* is
an historical novel set in a country in which the languages
spoken are French and Creole, and in which the culture of the
majority is of African origin. The subject of the novel therefore
demands a rich vocabulary. Yet, regardless of these conditions,
Carpentier deliberately exploits the potential of unfamiliar
language. As a result, the novel acquires some of the quality of
baroque prose, characterized by uncommon language or
unusual and striking images. The latter are also part of
Carpentier's style as the following examples show:

> El veneno se arrastraba por la Llanura del Norte, invadien-
> do los potreros y los establos. (47)
> ...los esclavos iban ennegreciendo lentamente la Plaza
> Mayor... (63)
> ...diez mulatas de enaguas azules piaban a todo trapo, en
> gran tremolina de hembras el viento. (74)
> De aquel agujero, negro como boca desdentada, brotaban
> de súbito unos alaridos... (142)

These characteristics of Carpentier's language, combined with
a tendency to write so that the narrative may be easily visualized,
give his prose the distinctive quality immediately noticed by the
reader. The extent to which it is derived from his emulation of
the baroque style of Spanish classical literature or from his own
conception of the baroque requires further examination. For the
moment, it is sufficient to conclude that the characteristics I

have mentioned indicate his intention, not only of describing America and its history vividly, but of exploiting a style he considers to be suited to the task.

6. Conclusion

Alejo Carpentier was in his forty-fifth year when *El reino de este mundo* was published in 1949. Although only his second novel, it was written at the beginning of a period of productive maturity that extended till his death in 1980 and included seven more novels and several short stories. As a relatively early yet mature work, it may therefore be adopted as a point of departure for considering his later fiction. This is not to suggest that the latter is inferior or that Carpentier was incapable of further innovation. Neither his craft as a writer nor his ideas remained unchanged after *El reino de este mundo*. But the novel was an achievement that he would not easily match in later work. It has, for example, a narrative economy and a cohesion that he surpassed only with the tightly integrated plot of *El acoso* (1956) and an acute sense of ironic humour that is equalled only in *El arpa y la sombra* (1979). Significantly enough, both novels, like *El reino de este mundo*, are among Carpentier's shorter works. In his longer novels these qualities are sustained only in *El recurso del método*. However, the justification for measuring Carpentier's later fiction against *El reino de este mundo* is a matter not of the relative merit of individual novels, but of the directions in his writing which, once established, were generally followed and developed in the remainder of his work. The uniqueness of Latin America, its history, and the theme of revolution continue to figure among his main preoccupations. The scope of his erudition, his meticulous use of sources, and the complexity of his language are a constant challenge to the reader and characterize most of his writing. His endeavour to understand and describe the nature of the relationship between America and Europe underlies several of his narratives and the plot of almost all his novels unfolds according to cyclical patterns. Above all, Carpentier retains the epic dimensions of *El reino de este mundo*. Although focused on characters who, like

Ti Noel, are involved in some of the major events of modern times or undertake epic journeys across oceans and continents, his narratives describe entire periods of history and deal with the progress of nations rather than individuals. Carpentier's methods and historical panoramas contribute significantly to his objective of promoting a narrative art intended to combat both the styles which he believed obscured an understanding of Latin America and the sense of inferiority which, in his opinion, marred the work of his predecessors. His own techniques allowed him not only to describe the idiosyncrasies of Latin American history and society in a manner he considered faithful to their character, but to show them as part of the broader context of world history. The success of his endeavour is succinctly, if somewhat offhandedly, summarized in a comment about him by the narrator of *Memorias del subdesarrollo* (1965) by the Cuban author Edmundo Desnoes: 'Como cronista de la barbarie americana no está mal; ha logrado sacar del subdesarrollo el paisaje y la absurda historia del Nuevo Mundo.'[11] Even allowing for the degree of cynical understatement that still emerges when taken out of context, the comment nonetheless fitly acknowledges the objective sought by Carpentier which he began to pursue in *El reino de este mundo*.

---

[11] Serie del Volador (México: Editorial Joaquín Mortíz, 1975), p.68.

Bibliographical Note

BOOKS

1. Arias, Salvador (ed.). *Recopilación de textos sobre Alejo Carpentier.* Serie Valoración Múltiple, La Habana: Casa de las Américas, 1977. Anthology of essays, extracts of reviews and comments. Contains a useful but incomplete bibliography of criticism. For articles relevant to *El reino de este mundo* see *14*, *20* and *22* below.

2. Barroso, Juan. *'Realismo mágico' y 'lo real maravilloso' en 'El reino de este mundo' y 'El siglo de las luces'.* Colección Polymita, Miami: Ediciones Universal, 1977. A slightly disjointed work. Studies the history and definition of the two terms. Analysis of *El reino de este mundo* also includes consideration of narrative technique and Voodoo as a major theme.

3. Bravo, José Antonio. *Lo real maravilloso en la narrativa latinoamericana actual: 'Cien años de soledad', 'El reino de este mundo', 'Pedro Páramo'.* Lima: Editoriales Unidas, 1978. Attempts a definition of 'lo real maravilloso' based on the prologue to *El reino de este mundo* but applicable to the contemporary Spanish American novel in general.

4. Carpentier, Alejo. *La música en Cuba.* Colección Popular, México: Fondo de Cultura Económica, 1972. Demonstrates the scope of Carpentier's knowledge of Caribbean history. Bibliography contains several references relevant for tracing the sources of *El reino de este mundo*.

5. Celorio, Gonzalo. *El surrealismo y lo real maravilloso americano.* Colección Sepsetentas, México: Secretaría de Educación Pública, 1976. A comparison between surrealist painting and contemporary Spanish American fiction. Some interesting insights, but lacks criteria for establishing differences among novelists.

6. Cole, Hubert. *Christophe, King of Haiti.* New York: The Viking Press, 1967. A good account, covering most of the period in which *El reino de este mundo* is set.

7. Giacoman, Helmy F. (ed.). *Homenaje a Alejo Carpentier: variaciones interpretativas en torno a su obra.* New York: Las Américas, 1970. Anthology of critical essays. See *20* and *26* below.

8. González Echevarría, Roberto. *Alejo Carpentier: The Pilgrim at Home.* Ithaca: Cornell University Press, 1977. Contains an illuminating chapter on the origins of Carpentier's ideas on literature and Latin America. Analysis of *El reino de este mundo*, however, is less convincing and is marred by occasional slips.

9. Márquez Rodríguez, Alexis. *La obra narrativa de Alejo Carpentier.* Caracas: Ediciones de la Biblioteca Central, Universidad Central de Venezuela, 1970. A general study of the life and work of Carpentier.

10. Mocega-González, Esther. *La narrativa de Alejo Carpentier: el concepto del tiempo como tema fundamental (ensayo de interpretación y análisis).* New York: Eliseo Torres and Sons, 1975. An elementary work. The chapter on *El reino de este mundo* re-tells the plot, dividing it into cycles based on the movements of the characters and the historical periods identified in the text.

11. Müller-Bergh, Klaus. *Alejo Carpentier: estudio biográfico crítico.* New York: Las Américas, 1972. Useful biography and chapter on Carpentier's early work. The bibliography includes an extensive, although incomplete, list of Carpentier's writings, including publications in periodicals and newspapers.

12. Müller-Bergh, Klaus (ed.). *Asedios a Carpentier: once ensayos críticos sobre el novelista cubano.* Santiago de Chile: Editorial Universitaria, 1972. Good anthology of essays, especially for Carpentier's early work (*¡Ecué-Yamba-O!, El reino de este mundo,* and short stories). See *21* and *23* below.

13. Sánchez-Boudy, José. *La temática novelística de Alejo Carpentier.* Miami: Ediciones Universal, 1969. The chapter on *El reino de este mundo* includes useful information on the historical context of the novel and a discussion of the themes of liberty and Voodoo.

ARTICLES

14. Cruz-Luis, Adolfo. 'Latinoamérica en Carpentier: génesis de lo real maravilloso', *Casa de las Américas,* XV, 87 (1974), 48-97. Also in *1,* pp.97-122, as 'De la raíz al fruto'. Traces the development of Carpentier's ideas on Latin America, principally through reference to his early publications in newspapers and periodicals.

15. Dávila Vázquez, Jorge. 'Barroco y magia en *El reino de este mundo*', *Cambio* (México), 9 (1977), 5-31. Includes a study of style in the novel, comparing it to aspects of the baroque based on criteria proposed by Helmut Hatzfeld (*Estudios sobre el barroco,* 2nd ed., Madrid: Gredos, 1966).

16. Fernández, Sergio. 'El destino de los dioses fuertes', *Diálogos* (México), XV, 85 (1979), 2-9. Contains brief observations on baroque style in *El reino de este mundo.*

17. Friedmann de Goldberg, Florinda. 'Estudio preliminar' in edition of *El reino de este mundo,* Buenos Aires: Librería del Colegio, 1975, pp.9-44. Good general introduction covering the major points of theme, structure, and narrative technique.

18. González Echevarría, Roberto. 'Isla a su vuelo fugitiva: Carpentier y el realismo mágico', *Revista Iberoamericana,* XL, 86 (1974), 9-63. Original Spanish version of the chapter 'Fugitive Island' in *8.*

19. Jitrik, Noé. 'Blanco, negro, ¿mulato? Una lectura de *El reino de este mundo,* de Alejo Carpentier', *Texto Crítico,* I, 1 (1975), 32-60. Occasionally difficult but gives useful insight on the structure and meaning of the novel.

20. Leante, César. 'Confesiones sencillas de un escritor barroco', *1,* pp.57-70, and *7,* pp.11-31. An important interview, frequently cited by critics. Carpentier speaks of the origin of his works, his early life, intellectual formation and the influence of Surrealism.

21. Müller-Bergh, Klaus. 'Corrientes vanguardistas y surrealismo en la obra de Alejo Carpentier', *Revista Hispánica Moderna*, XXXV (1969), 323-40. Also in *12*, pp.13-38. The first part examines the development of Carpentier's ideas about Latin America, referring to articles published in *Social* and *Carteles* and his association with the *Grupo minorista* in Cuba and Surrealism in Paris. The second part deals with *Los pasos perdidos*.

22. Rincón, Carlos. 'Sobre Alejo Carpentier y la poética de lo real maravilloso', *Casa de las Américas*, XV, 89 (1975), 40-65. Also in *1*, pp.123-77. Outlines the history of the marvellous from European Classicism to Surrealism and Carpentier's application of the term to Latin America with a meaning that opposes the surrealist notion of 'le merveilleux'.

23. Rodríguez Monegal, Emir. 'Lo real y lo maravilloso en *El reino de este mundo*', *Revista Iberoamericana*, XXXVII, 76-7 (1971), 619-49. Also in *12*, pp.101-32. Well-documented account of Carpentier's involvement with Surrealism. Discusses the prologue and the novel as a reaction to the movement. Commentary in the second part of the article includes examples of how the marvellous is obtained in the text, but should be read in conjunction with more recent criticism.

24. Speratti-Piñero, Emma Susana. 'Noviciado y apoteosis de Ti Noel en *El reino de este mundo*, de Alejo Carpentier', *Bulletin Hispanique*, LXXX (1978), 201-28. Discusses the novel in the light of the development of the character of Ti Noel. Provides much useful information on sources and Voodoo.

25. Volek, Emil. 'Realismo mágico: notas sobre su génesis y naturaleza en Alejo Carpentier', *Nueva Narrativa Hispanoamericana*, III, 2 (1973), 257-74. Comparison of 'lo real maravilloso' with the principal elements of Surrealism and discussion of Carpentier's approach to the description of reality in the light of its relation to German Expressionism.

26. ——. 'Análisis e interpretación de *El reino de este mundo*, de Alejo Carpentier', in *7*, pp.145-78. One of the basic pieces of criticism. From an analysis of the artistic structure of the novel, Volek argues that elements of realism, the marvellous, and Surrealism are subordinated to Carpentier's conception of history.